Report Of The Scientific Results Of The Voyage Of S.y. "scotia" During The Years 1902, 1903, And 1904: Under The Leadership Of William S. Bruce ..., Volume 4, Issue 1...

Scottish National Antarctic Expedition, 1902-1904

REPORT

ON THE

SCIENTIFIC RESULTS

OF THE

VOYAGE OF S.Y. "SCOTIA"

SCENE OFF COATS LAND, ANTARCTICA.

WEDDELL SEALS AND EMPEROR PENGUINS.

SCOTTISH NATIONAL ANTARCTIC EXPEDITION.

REPORT

ON THE

SCIENTIFIC RESULTS

OF THE

VOYAGE OF S.Y. "SCOTIA"

DURING THE YEARS 1902, 1903, AND 1904,

UNDER THE LEADERSHIP OF

WILLIAM S. BRUCE,

LL.D., F.R.S.E.

Volume IV.—ZOOLOGY.

PART I.—ZOOLOGICAL LOG, by David W. Wilton, J. H. Harvey Pirie, B.Sc., M.D., etc., and R. N. Rudmose Brown, B.Sc.

Thirty-three Plates and two Maps,
including 100 *Photographs by* The Editor *and* The Authors.
Coloured Frontispiece by William Smith.

EDINBURGH:

𝕿𝖍𝖊 𝕾𝖈𝖔𝖙𝖙𝖎𝖘𝖍 𝕺𝖈𝖊𝖆𝖓𝖔𝖌𝖗𝖆𝖕𝖍𝖎𝖈𝖆𝖑 𝕷𝖆𝖇𝖔𝖗𝖆𝖙𝖔𝖗𝖞.

SOLD AT

THE SCOTTISH OCEANOGRAPHICAL LABORATORY;
JAMES THIN, 55 SOUTH BRIDGE, EDINBURGH;
JAMES MACLEHOSE & SONS, 61 ST VINCENT STREET, GLASGOW.

1908.

Price Thirteen Shillings in cloth; Ten Shillings and Sixpence in paper.

EDITORIAL NOTE.

ON previous voyages I had learnt the value of keeping immediate records in a systematic manner of everything of scientific value, so that memory need never be trusted to, even for the matter of a day, and so that things observed could be referred to at any time in black and white. To Mr DAVID W. WILTON I handed over the keeping of the Zoological Log, and I cannot praise too highly the systematic and conscientious manner in which he gathered us all together every evening and extracted from us in brief everything we had seen during the day of zoological interest. While, therefore, the log is his excellent work, it is the summing up of everything that was noted during every day. I may mention that the crew became keen and accurate observers and careful collectors, and to them are due many most valuable records. Among all the ship's company there was, perhaps, no better observer than our second officer, the late Mr ROBERT DAVIDSON. He would distinguish a new bird on the wing at long distance before anybody on board.

From the start of the Scottish National Antarctic Expedition to its finish the open-air observations of the naturalists on board were recorded daily in this log. The log makes no pretensions to being anything more than a field note-book of the natural history of the voyage. It was, naturally, impossible to identify all birds seen on the wing, and all marine animals passed by when the ship was making passages from one point to another. In consequence, especially during the passage of the "Scotia" through the tropics, the records on many days are slight; and if the entries occasionally have little scientific value, they can at least claim to be a faithful record of life observed. During the "Scotia's" cruises in antarctic seas, and more particularly during her wintering in Scotia Bay, South Orkneys, the daily entries will be found to be fuller and more precise, and it is from those regions that the observations will have most value. Everyone on board was conversant with the names of the antarctic birds and seals; the attention of all the naturalists was concentrated on the work; and since the "Scotia" was then in her special field of operations, there was seldom, if ever, any attempt made at quick passages. The log, therefore, expanded from a few cursory observations into a detailed naturalists' diary.

The log has been prepared for publication with no material alterations; the names of the animals referred to have been added in footnotes wherever possible and desirable, and here and there a few explanatory notes have been inserted at the bottom of the page. Otherwise it stands exactly as it was written from day to day.

While Mr D. W. WILTON was the recorder for by far the greater part of the voyage, it was occasionally necessary for him, during his absence on sledge and boat journeys, to delegate the task to another member of the scientific staff, usually Mr R. N. RUDMOSE BROWN; when this was the case it has been recorded in a note. During the summer months of 1903–04, when the "Scotia" was absent coaling and refitting at the Falkland Islands and Buenos Aires, Dr J. H. HARVEY PIRIE was the author of the "Zoological Log of Omond House, Scotia Bay."

I have to thank Mr R. N. RUDMOSE BROWN for the very great help he has given me in the editing of this part of Volume IV.; I have also been aided by Professor J. ARTHUR THOMSON and Mrs BRUCE in the final revision of the proofs. The work is greatly enhanced by the coloured frontispiece of Mr WILLIAM SMITH, of Aberdeen, doubly valuable since he has had experience as artist in a Polar expedition. I have to cordially thank Messrs BLACKWOOD for the use of blocks for no less than fifteen of the illustrations, which have previously appeared in their interesting publication entitled *The Voyage of the Scotia*, and Messrs ROWLAND WARD for allowing their photograph of the great sea-lion to appear.

WILLIAM S. BRUCE,
Editor.

CONTENTS.

ZOOLOGICAL LOG OF "SCOTIA."

ZOOLOGICAL LOG OF THE SUMMER STATION, OMOND HOUSE.

LIST OF ILLUSTRATIONS AND MAPS.

b

LIST OF ILLUSTRATIONS.

FACING PAGE

PART I.—ZOOLOGICAL LOG.

Zoological Log of Scottish National Antarctic Expedition.

R. N. Rudmose Brown.　　　David W. Wilton.　　J. H. Harvey Pirie.　　[Photo by W. S. Bruce.

2. *In medias res.*—The "Scotia" Naturalists, Messrs Wilton, Brown, and Pirie, in the "Scotia" Deck Laboratory.

Weddell Island.　　　　　　Saddle Island.

[Photo by W. S. Bruce.

3. Saddle Island, South Orkneys, as seen looking North-West from Jessie Bay, where the "Scotia"
Naturalists made their first Antarctic Landing.

ZOOLOGICAL LOG OF S.Y. SCOTIA, 1902-04

DAVID W. WILTON,
Recorder.

Nov. 11th, 50° 46′ N. 7° 35′ W.—A lark flew on board about noon, and though we took great care of it, it succumbed to exhaustion during the night.

Nov. 13th, 46° 20′ N. 10° 00′ W.—Sharks were observed for the first time this afternoon while we were engaged in kite-flying.

Nov. 16th, 40° 45′ N. 13° 16′ W.—Gulls seen during the day.

Nov. 17th, 39° 34′ N. 14° 01′ W.—Birds observed in the afternoon too far off to make out.

Nov. 18th, 36° 59′ N. 14° 34′ W.—Two gulls seen.

Nov. 19th, 34° 18′ N. 15° 25′ W.—Stormy petrels observed at 10 A.M.

Nov. 20th, Arrived at Funchal, Madeira, 9 A.M.—Crows, sparrow-hawks, corbies and pigeons seen during our stay. Botanical and zoological collections on shore and land were made. A large number of species of fish were bought at the market and sent home. Several of the scientific staff went by rail about 2000 feet up for collecting and secured some lizards, butterflies and a small collection of plants. Lizards are to be seen everywhere, even in houses. Pirie did some shore collecting.

Nov. 24th, 30° 14′ N. 18° 13′ W.—First of Mother Carey's chickens seen to-day.

Nov. 25th, 28° 14′ N. 19° 15′ W.—Several petrels observed during the day.

Nov. 26th, 26° 23′ N. 20° 20′ W.—Shark and petrels seen. First tow-net taken by Brown contained *Appendicularia* and bright blue copepods. The third one came up torn, and the marks upon it seem to point to a shark.

Nov. 27th, 24° 21′ N. 21° 20′ W.—Petrels seen. A specimen of *Halobates* was taken in the tow-net for the first time.

Nov. 28th, 21° 58′ N. 22° 26′ W.—Petrels seen. Radiolarians very plentiful in the tow-net.

Nov. 29th, 20° 18′ N. 23° 22′ W.—Petrels seen. *Halobates* and *Sagitta* in the tow-net.

A

Nov. 30th, 18° 59′ N. 24° 20′ W.—First flying-fish [1] observed. Preserved four which flew on board. *Pulvinulina* in abundance in the tow-net.

Dec. 1st, At Porto Grande, St Vincent, Cape Verde Islands.—Shark seen outside harbour. Pirie went collecting along the shore and brought back a good collection. We bought several species of fish at the market. A very barren place, and the only bird seen was a buzzard, which people here say act as scavengers of the place and are protected by law. Peridineans observed in tow-net.

Dec. 2nd, 15° 15′ N. 25° 09′ W.—Petrels and flying-fish observed all day long, the latter seem to flutter their wings and change the direction of their flight.[2]

Dec. 3rd, 13° 07′ N. 25° 09′ W.—Several boobies, petrels, flying-fish, bonitos and dolphins seen ; the last two for the first time.

Dec. 4th, 11° 15′ N. 25° 20′ W.—Several boobies, petrels, flying-fish and bonitos seen during the day. Caught two bonitos and dissected one—preserved the other. Some small *Physalia* in the tow-net.

Dec. 5th, 9° 23′ N. 25° 31′ W.—Caught a shark soon after noon, dimensions of which were taken. Sample of liver, brain, etc., of the shark preserved, also two sucker fish adhering to it. *Halobates* observed in tow-net ; blue copepods plentiful.

Dec. 6th, 7° 35′ N. 25° 32′ W.—Flying-fish and petrels observed.

Dec. 7th, 5° 25′ N. 26° 07′ W.—Flying-fish and petrels. Fitchie pointed out fins of some whales far off. Portuguese men-of-war also seen. *Halobates* very plentiful in tow-net, and copepods remarkably scarce.

Dec. 8th, 3° 13′ N. 26° 30′ W.—Flying-fish and petrels seen. Large flashes of phosphorescence observed at night. Many light blue copepods in tow-net.

Dec. 9th, 1° 42′ N. 27° 32′ W.—Flying-fish and petrels seen. Caught some specimens of *Velella* whilst kite was out.

Dec. 10th, St. Paul's Rocks, 0° 55′ N. 29° 22′ W.—Sharks innumerable. Secured eight specimens, and took dimensions and weight of each, besides preserving one whole, and the heads of two others, one especially for brains and nerves. A school of porpoises seen about 8 A.M. Tried to effect a landing on the rocks, but the high sea running at the time foiled our attempts. Several fish seen but none caught, as the sharks took every bait. Plenty of boobies[3] and terns[4] on the rocks. Observed some boobies nesting : the young ones nearly white. Shot some adult birds of each kind but could not get any young. *Physalia* seen. *Velella* frequently seen and we secured also planarians and some kind of spawn on a dead *Velella*.

Dec. 11th, 0° 22′ S. 31° 00′ W.—Flying-fish and petrels observed. Tow-net catch very poor, except for foraminifers.

Dec. 12th, 2° 01′ S. 32° 18′ W.—The first large *Physalia* seen this afternoon. A couple of boobies also observed and flying-fish seen in great quantities.

---

[1] *Exocetus volitans.*

[2] Observations were made daily on board to attempt to settle the question as to whether or not the flying-fish can use their pectoral fins as functional wings.

[3] *Sula leucogaster.*   [4] *Anous stolidus* and *Micranous leucocapillus.*

Zoological Log of Scottish National Antarctic Expedition.

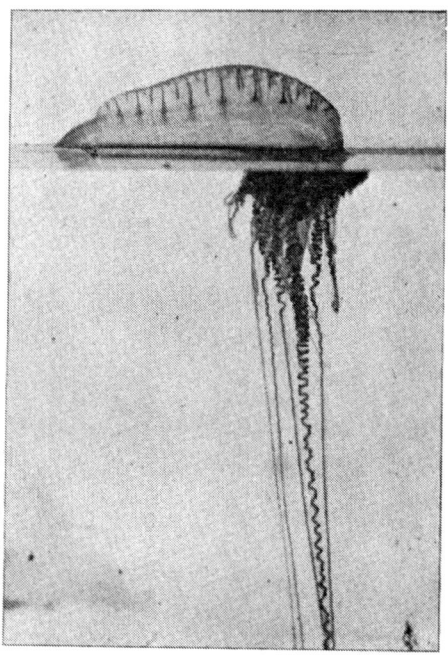

4. Full Sail! [Photo by W. S. Bruce.

[Photo by W. S. Bruce.

5. End Tilted Up whilst Turning Over!

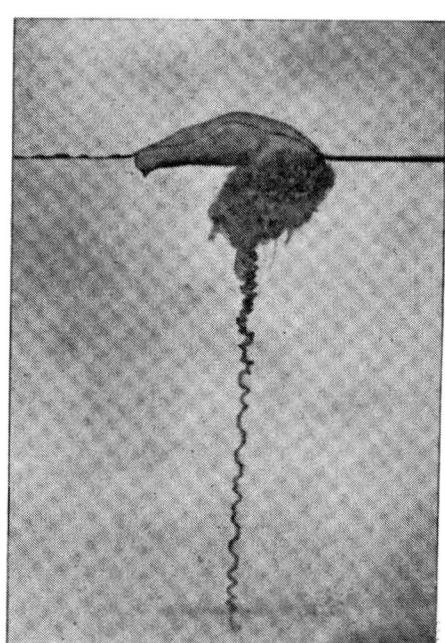

[Photo by W. S. Bruce.

6. Lying!

Portuguese Man-o'-War (*Physalia*). (¼ natural size.)

Dec. 13th, 3° 38′ S. 33° 20′ W.—Observed some specimens of *Physalia*, *Velella*, and flying - fish before breakfast. Mr Bruce, Brown and myself saw a gannet about noon, white with black tips on its wings. Saw a bird in the afternoon, which looked like a petrel, too far off to determine. Radiolarians very plentiful in tow-net.

Dec. 14th, 5° 50′ S. 34° 20′ W.—What the captain describes as "dolphin whales"[1] were seen this morning, when a dozen or more of these cetaceans were lying lazily on the surface of the water, and, though the ship passed within 50 yards of them, they paid no attention to it. Their colour seemed to be a greyish black. A flock of birds (skuas) were seen by Mr Bruce and the captain in the afternoon, of a black colour except belly and breast which were white, but they were too far off to distinguish clearly. In the afternoon saw the coast of Brazil near Pernambuco. Very few crustaceans observed in tow-net.

Dec. 15th, 7° 20′ S. 34° 38′ W.—Saw a large turtle this afternoon off the coast whilst we were out in a boat kite-flying; we tried to capture it, with no success. Two kinds of small fish seen in tow-net, a pearl-fish and a young pipe-fish. A number of porpoises seen in the evening.

Dec. 16th, 9° 6′ S. 34° 38′ W.—Saw two boobies in morning whilst after kite. A sucker fish, one inch long, observed in tow-net, also two species of gasteropods and one young lamellibranch, but crustaceans are still comparatively scarce.

Dec. 17th, 11° 28′ S. 35° 50′ W.—Flying-fish seen in considerable numbers. Saw a large *Physalia* before breakfast. Mr Bruce and Pirie saw a brownish speckly bird, like a young herring gull. Crustaceans still scarce in the plankton.

Dec. 18th, 13° 26′ S. 36° 45′ W.—Several flying-fish seen to-day. A small bird was observed this evening of a black colour and the size of a thrush. Crustaceans still scarce in the tow-net.

Dec. 19th, 15° 24′ S. 37° 12′ W.—Flying-fish still to the fore. A flock of dark coloured birds like noddies, and two white ones, were seen this morning. After dinner Mr Bruce caught a large *Physalia*, which was drawn and painted. Other specimens were also seen.

Dec. 20th, 18° 11′ S. 37° 55′ W.—We had a dredge out for the first time to-day at 15.30 to 16 hours,[2] in 36 fathoms coral bottom, 18° 26′ S. 37° 58′ W.; 138½ fathoms of steel rope were paid out, and a pressure of about a quarter of a ton was registered on the dynomometer. We steamed very slowly ahead, trailing the dredge along the bottom for thirty-five minutes. The following list shows the groups represented in the contents :—

Foraminifera	Porifera	Hydroidea
Alcyonaria	Pennatulidæ	"Corals"

[1] It is impossible to give the names of Antarctic cetaceans with any degree of accuracy until specimens are secured and a definite study of these undertaken.

[2] This dredging was taken on the Abrolhos Bank.

Polychaeta	Bryozoa	Ophiuroidea
Crinoidea	*Caprella*	Decapoda
Mollusca		

These animals were mostly attached to the two swabs fastened to the dredge. The dredge itself was torn.

Several large specimens of *Physalia* were seen during the time the dredge was out, one of which was caught.

Dec. 21st, 20° 40′ S. 38° 20′ W.—Flying-fish and a large *Physalia* observed in the morning.

Dec. 22nd, 22° 42′ S. 39° 22′ W.—Flying-fish and *Physalia*. A small dark bird (the size of a sparrow) was seen flying over the bridge. Gasteropods (1-2m.m. shell) abundant in tow-net. Sea very phosphorescent to-night.

Dec. 23rd, 24° 42′ S. 40° 34′ W.—Largest shoal of flying-fish seen during the voyage passed after breakfast. One *Halobates* in tow-net to-day.

Dec. 24th, 26° 35′ S. 42° 05′ W.—A black petrel, a booby and two gulls seen by the captain. Flying-fish still plentiful. Copepods again abundant in tow-net.

Dec. 25th, 28° 27′ S. 43° 45′ W.—Petrels, boobies and flying-fish seen after lunch. Dirty grey yellowish threshers (fully 20 ft.) were seen jumping clean out of the water as a large school of them passed by, travelling in a south-easterly direction.

Dec. 26th, 30° 25′ S. 45° 45′ W.—A petrel with a white breast and belly, a brownish black colour generally and a small white marking on the under and upper surface of the wing, has been seen for the last two or three days. Mr Bruce believes it to be of the prion family. Its dimensions approximate to those of *Fulmar glacialis* but its wings appear to be sharper: several were seen to-day. A small petrel was also observed which may be Wilson's petrel.[1] Its plumage is mainly black but it has a white belt right round the rump. Apparently the captain also saw it yesterday. Flying-fish observed this morning and a booby was seen after dinner. Copepods plentiful in tow-net.

Dec. 27th, 32° 15′ S. 47° 30′ W.—A large number of moths were observed during the day, and specimens of about three different species were caught.[2] No flying-fish have been seen to-day by anyone on board. A *Velella* was caught and a fine specimen of *Doliolum* was seen. Prion petrel and Wilson's petrel also seen. A *Physalia* caught but its accompanying fish was not captured.[3]

Dec. 28th, 33° 50′ S. 48° 44′ W.—A thresher was seen this morning. About 2.30 P.M. a long band of brownish scum was observed floating on the surface of the water.[4] The position of this band was 34° 02′ S. 49° 07′ W. A boat put off to collect samples of this scum and to shoot birds (prion petrels) which were hovering around us. Several animals were discovered amongst this floating mass and fine specimens of

---

[1] *Oceanites oceanicus.*   [2] These moths were blown from the land by an offshore breeze. We were at the time 80 to 90 miles off the Brazilian coast.   [3] A species of small fish generally accompanies the *Physalia.*   [4] *Trichodesmium erythraeum.*

Zoological Log of Scottish National Antarctic Expedition.

[*Photo by T. C. Day.*

7. Large Sunfish (*Orthagoriscus mola*) in Scottish Oceanographical Laboratory, captured lat. 39° 01′ S., long. 53° 40′ W.

(*A*)

(*B*)

[*Photo by T. C. Day.*

8. Sucking-fish (*Echeneis*) taken alive inside the mouth of the Sunfish. (⅓ natural size.)
(*A*) Dorsal Aspect, showing Sock on Top of Head.   (*B*) Ventral Aspect.

a species of medusoid[1] and *Physalia* were captured. Fish, *Cydippe*, amphipods and *Doliolum* were also secured. Four specimens of *Salpa* were also obtained inside three petrels which were shot. Large phosphorescent flashes similar to those of an electric arc lamp were seen at night. A turtle was seen this morning.

Dec. 29th, 35° 28′ S. 50° 34′ W.—Martin saw flying-fish at 2 A.M. from the fo'c'sle head skimming along the water. A thresher and a finner were seen this morning quite close to each other; the thresher was observed to jump out of the water. Another variety of prion petrel observed during the afternoon by Mr Bruce and others, almost entirely white on the under surface, white throat probably up to beak, white breast and belly, white also under tail except probably at the tip, and white under the wings; the rest very like the prion shot yesterday. Prion petrels and a small petrel very like Wilson's observed. Crustaceans almost absent in tow-net which contained a number of examples of *Salpa*.

Dec. 30th, 35° 23′ S. 49° 53′ W.—Wilson's petrel and several petrels of the two prion kinds and two albatroses hovered about the ship for the greater part of the day. The last named birds seen for the first time.

Dec. 31st, 36° 39′ S. 52° 10′ W.—Same birds observed as yesterday. *Salpa* very abundant in tow-net.

Jan. 1st 1903, 39° 01′ S. 53° 40′ W.—Wilson's petrels, two kinds of prion petrels, albatroses and a bosun bird were observed to-day. Sun-fish[2] were also seen : at 2.30 P.M. a boat was lowered to get one. After several ineffective attempts at harpooning we managed to stun one with shot. Davidson after a while drove the harpoon into the gills, and we then made fast to one of its fins and towed it to the ship. Three or four sucker fish accompanied it to the boat, and on cutting the sun-fish up, one was discovered in the gills. A parasitic copepod *(Argulus)* was found externally, as well as a polyclad. There was also a parasitic copepod on the gills and a barnacle on the lip. In the intestines numerous tape-worms were found and another leech-like parasite. There was in all probably about 10 lbs. weight of tape-worms in the gut. Its weight by the dynomometer was half a ton. Several others were seen twice as large. Brown saw a globe-fish with a small fish attendant on it. *Salpa* were seen frequently floating past. Specimens of *Salpa* still in tow-net. Jelly fish the same as secured in the *Trichodesmium* band were observed floating past. Liver and heart of the sun-fish preserved as well as the skin.

Jan. 3rd, 45° 29′ S. 56° 03′ W.—At 6 A.M. Mr Bruce observed a whale and a bird like a gull, but too distant to identify. The other birds seen were the same as yesterday. This afternoon whilst sounding, a bird like a Cape pigeon was observed by Mr Bruce though it was darker and fatter; it was probably the same as that seen in distance this morning. Whales seen at 10 A.M. by the captain. Davidson caught a moth during tea-time, whilst setting the mizzen. Barnacles were found by Brown on a piece of seaweed.[3] Pink copepods *(cf. Calanus)* in 9 A.M. tow-net.

---

[1] *Phacellophora ornata.*   [2] *Orthagoriscus mola.*   [3] Probably the southern kelp, *Macrocystis pyrifera.*

Jan. 4th, 47° 37′ S. 57° 25′ W.—Penguins[1] seen for the first time this afternoon. The captain saw a sooty albatros.[2] The prion with the white under surface has entirely replaced the one with only the breast and abdomen white : the colour on the dorsal surface of this bird is mainly in two shades, dark, almost black, at the tips of the wings verging into grey on the rest of the body with a white ring round neck and tail. Two finners were seen this morning. Long tentacles[3] from 60 to 100 feet were caught on the sounding wire at about 1000 fathoms depth. Wilson's petrels very plentiful. A large school of porpoises, black on the back and white on the belly, probably same species as those seen by Mr Bruce in 1892[4] in about the same latitude, and at Port Stanley, were seen playing under the bows of the ship at 8.45 P.M. (The skeleton of the porpoise caught in 1892 is to be seen in the museum of University College, Dundee.) Phosphorescence not so marked during the last two nights.

Jan. 5th, 49° 55′ S. 57° 44′ W.—Two albatroses and several white prions seen. The morning was rather misty and no birds were observed.

Jan. 6th, Dropped anchor at Port Stanley, Falkland Islands at 8 a.m.—Steamer ducks[5] and black-backed gulls[6] numerous in the harbour. A trap was put down this evening.

Jan. 7th to Jan. 25th, Port Stanley.—During our stay at Port Stanley several excursions were made by the various members of the staff and a small trap was set each day in the harbour and a big one let down in 6 fathoms in Port William, which we took up on our way out. Two species of mammal were seen ; a seal[7] and porpoises. Several specimens of birds were secured, viz., the rock or kelp goose *(Chloëphaga hybrida)*; the logger-headed duck or goose, also known as the steamer duck ; a heron-like bird called a king-quawk,[8] white breasted oyster catchers,[9] shags,[10] a jackass penguin,[11] the ringed dotterel,[12] a snipe[13] resembling the jack-snipe, two species of sand-pipers,[14] a linnet with a greenish plumage, a bird resembling a white throat[15] and a black oyster catcher,[16] whilst the black-backed gull *(Larus dominicanus),* the hawk known as the "johnnie rook,"[17] and a thrush[18] were seen. Mr Thomson kindly gave us a collection of eggs. Two fishes were bought from a fisherman and sent home ; several were also obtained in the traps. Of invertebrates quite a considerable number of specimens were obtained by means of the trap and inland excursions. Miss Blyth presented the expedition with some shells and Mr Coulson, Junr., of Cape Pembroke Lighthouse, gave us some birds and other animals picked up at the lighthouse.

Jan. 26th.—Left Port Stanley in the morning and picked up the big trap at Port William. In the trap were some fishes, several molluscs, including an octopus, some holothurians and other echinoderms.

---

[1] Probably *Spheniscus magellanicus* of the Falklands.   [2] Probably *Phoebetria cornicoides.*
[3] The tentacles of a Siphonophore.   [4] During his cruise in the Dundee whaler *Balaena.*
[5] *Tachyeres cinereus.*   [6] *Larus dominicanus.*   [7] *Arctocephalus (?) Falklandicus.*
[8] *Nycticorax obscurus (N. tayazu-guira).*   [9] *Haematopus leucopus.*   [10] *Phalacrocorax atriceps* and *P. albiventer.*   [11] *Spheniscus magellanicus.*   [12] *Endromias modesta.*   [13] *Gallinago paraguayae.*
[14] *Tringa fuscicollis.*   [15] *Muscisaxicola macloviana.*   [16] *Haematopus ater.*
[17] *Milvago australis.*   [18] *Turdus falklandicus.*

Zoological Log of Scottish National Antarctic Expedition.

[Photo by W. S. Bruce.

10. Securing a Shot Oyster Catcher near Cape Pembroke, Falkland Islands.

12. Sea Elephant (*Macrorhinus leoninus*), Port William, Falkland Islands.

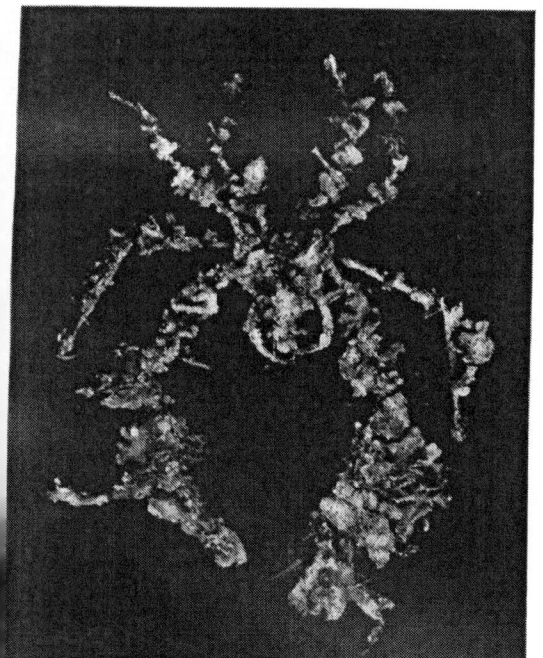

[Photo by T. C. Day.

9. Crab masked with Red Algæ, Sponges, etc., from Abrolhos Bank; 36 fathoms; lat. 18° 28′ S., long. 37° 58′ W. (1½ natural size.)

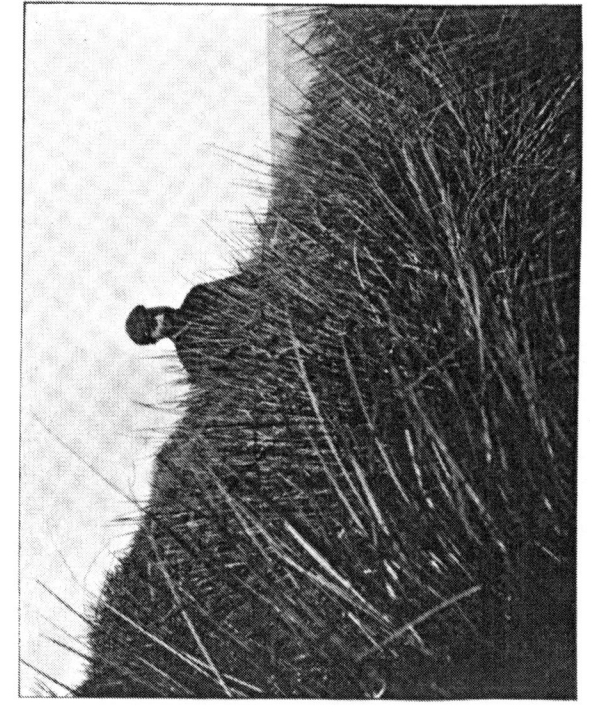

[Photo by W. S. Bruce.

11. Tussock Grass (*Dactylis cæspitosa*), where Sea-lions sleep. Tussock Islands, near Port Stanley, Falkland Islands.

Jan. 27th, 52° 55′ S. 55° 00′ W.—Several porpoises (black and white) seen. Albatros,[1] Wilson's petrels and blue petrels[2] were also observed, the latter for the first time. Sea very phosphorescent at night.

Jan. 28th, 54° 35′ S. 51° 50′ W.—Wilson's petrels and albatroses were seen.

Jan. 29th, 56° 10′ S. 49° 20′ W.—Albatros, sooty albatros, molliemauk,[3] Wilson's and blue petrels seen. A strong gale was blowing all day. Very little phosphorescence to-night.

Jan. 30th, 56° 28′ S. 47° 52′ W.—Albatros, sooty albatros,[4] molliemauk, Wilson's and blue petrels seen ; also Cape pigeons[5] for the first time.

Jan. 31st, 58° 14′ S. 45° 15′ W.—Same birds as yesterday. Finners and bottle-noses plentiful. Long yellow nemertean worm found on sounding wire.

Feb. 1st, 59° 32′ S. 43° 10′ W.—Sooty albatros and molliemauks (grey and greyish black with no white) blue and Wilson's petrels observed. Cape pigeons of which four specimens were secured by means of a landing net during sounding, and a penguin[6] (jackass or antarctic) were also seen to-day. Finners were seen in great numbers.

Feb. 2nd, 60° 28′ S. 43° 40′ W.—Saw our first seal lying on a piece of ice about 100 yards distant from the edge of the pack. Many others were seen during the day and in the evening. Pirie shot two, one of which, a male, was taken on board. Nearly all the seals are *Lobodon carcinophaga*.[7] One piece of ice was covered with red fæces probably caused by the seals feeding on *Euphausia*, which also forms part of Cape pigeons' diet. A few sea-leopards (*Stenorhynchus leptonyx*) were also seen, as well as several finners. As to birds, the same were observed as yesterday. Two flocks of black-headed terns with grey backs and white underneath[8] were observed by Mr Bruce sitting on the ice. These and snowy petrels[9] and antarctic penguins[10] were noticed for the first time. A flock of the latter were sitting on an iceberg, and some were seen in the water. What was probably a sheathbill[11] on the wing was noted by the leader. Two Cape pigeons, a brace of snowy petrels and a Wilson's petrel were secured. The blue petrels seem to diminish in numbers the further one gets into the ice. The captain noticed a white sooty albatros.[12] Red schizopods (*Euphausia*) were very plentiful between the ice floes. Two compound ascidians were also seen, probably the same as obtained in 1892.[13] Some of the sailors reported a few small fishes. A great deal of ice which we passed was covered with a yellowish tinge about the water line doubtless caused by diatoms.

Feb. 3rd, 60° 23′ S. 44° 00′ W.—No blue petrels seen to-day. A young albatros appeared in sight at 8 P.M. Mr Bruce observed a bird like a skua. Silver[14] and giant petrels[15] seen for the first time ; other birds the same as yesterday. Two kinds of

[1] *Diomedea exulans.*   [2] Probably *Prion banksi.*   [3] *Thalassogeron chlororhynchus.*
[4] Probably *Phoebetria fuliginosa.*   [5] *Daption capensis.*
[6] Probably *Pygoscelis antarctica.*   [7] The white seal or crab-eater.   [8] *Sterna hirundinacea.*
[9] *Pagodroma nivea.*   [10] *Pygoscelis antarctica.*   [11] *Chionis alba.*   [12] Probably *Ossifraga gigantea.*
[13] During the cruise of the *Balaena.*   [14] *Priocella glacialoides.*   [15] *Ossifraga gigantea.*

penguins were noticed (*Pygoscelis antarctica* and *P. adelia*), also two sheathbills. Plenty of young seals (*Lobodon*) were observed swimming about. They seemed to evince a great curiosity on the ship's approach, came quite close, diving from one side to the other, and were constantly popping their heads up and taking a good look at us. The small petrel which we have been calling Wilson's or stormy, a specimen of which was shot yesterday, we found to be Wilson's stormy petrel (*Oceanites oceanicus*). The penguins showed a great interest at our arrival, swimming after us in their funny porpoise fashion, so that at first sight one is apt to consider them as anything but birds. Their position on the ice is either lying down or squatting; when walking they assume a very droll appearance, maintaining a gait something like an old salt would after a very long voyage. In diving and jumping on to the ice they show remarkable agility, taking leaps of about 5 feet or more from the water on to the floe; sometimes they miss their foothold and roll back into the sea. Some examples of *Euphausia* were collected.

Feb. 4th, 60° 47′ S. 44° 00′ W.—At 8 A.M. a landing was made on the north east side of Saddle Island. There is a large penguin rookery (*Pygoscelis antarctica*) on the Isle. Specimens of sheathbills and young, young and adult penguins, large brown skuas[1] and young, and young Cape pigeons were secured, whilst albatroses, giant petrels, shags[2] and a gull were seen. The eggs of penguins were obtained. Whilst unearthing stones for a cairn, we found some collembolids[3] and acarinids, which seem to be very plentiful. Mr Bruce observed some red anemones whilst nearing land, and also a calcareous growth (alga) on the rocks below water. Terns, Cape pigeons, Wilson's, and snowy petrels also seen during the day. Compound ascidians, finners, seals and probably a sea-elephant (*Macrorhinus leoninus*).[4]

Feb. 5th, 61° 06′ S. 43° 40′ W.—Molliemauks, Wilson's petrels, Cape pigeons, black-throate., nged and gentoo penguins seen to-day. Mr Bruce saw a compound ascidian. No beasts have been observed in the tow-net since we left the Falkland Islands, the catch consisting almost solely of diatoms. Finner whales and *Lobodons* were very conspicuous to-day.

Feb. 6th, 60° 10′ S. 42° 35′ W.—A female Ross seal (*Ommatophoca rossi*) was shot by Pirie this morning before breakfast. It was found lying on a small floe, and allowed the ship to come within twenty yards of it without moving. Its temperature was 96°·2. On opening its stomach a fairly complete cuttlefish, and two beaks, several large examples of *Euphausia*, and a fish resembling a whiting were found. Cestodes and nematodes were present in the stomach and gut. The sea-leopard was frequently met with during the day as well as several finners. Many *Euphausia* were frequently observed, and it was noticed after dark that these caused a phosphorescence on the ice and in the water.

Most of the day we have been sailing in open water away from the pack, and we

---

[1] *Megalestris antarctica.*   [2] *Phalacrocorax atriceps.*   [3] *Cryptopygus crassus.*
[4] A specimen of this animal was certainly seen in Scotia Bay in April 1904.

Zoological Log of Scottish National Antarctic Expedition.

[Photo by W. S. Bruce.

13. Weddell Seal (*Leptonychotes weddelli*).

[Photo by R. N. R. Brown.

14. White Antarctic Seal (*Lobodon carcinophaga*).

[Photo by J. H. H. Pirie.

15. Sea Leopard Seal (*Stenorhynchus leptonyx*).

[Photo by W. S. Bruce.

16. Ross Seal (*Ommatophoca rossi*).

again fell in with the blue petrel.[1] Cape pigeons, Wilson's petrels, molliemauks, sheathbills and snowy petrels followed in the ship's wake at different times.

Feb. 7th, 60° 03′ S. 39° 44′ W.—A great host of nellies or giant petrels, Cape pigeons and stormy petrels feeding on carcase of dead whale at 5 A.M. Nellies white to nearly black. Snowy, Wilson's and blue petrels, Cape pigeons and a nelly were seen during the remainder of the day. Rather foggy all day, and very few birds were seen. A small fish resembling a sardine, in a very mangled condition, probably about 3 inches in length was found in the oesophagus of Ross's seal which was captured yesterday. *Lobodons* (both light and dark) and *Stenorhynchus* were met with to-day. A large quantity of *Euphausia* was observed on the tongues of pack ice.

Feb. 8th, 59° 44′ S. 36° 40′ W.—Birds were not seen to-day in such quantities as on previous days, which may be accounted for by the morning being rather dull, though in the afternoon it cleared up ; perhaps there was no food for them among the closer pack. Cape pigeons, Wilson's petrels, blue prions and snowy petrels and paddies or sheathbills were the only birds observed. Finners conspicuous. *Euphausia* still among honeycombed ice.

Feb. 9th, 59° 42′ S. 34° 13′ W.—Mr Bruce observed a seal early this morning following the ship's wake, popping its head to port then diving and coming up on the starboard. Pirie shot another seal (*Stenorhynchus leptonyx*) whose skin and skull we preserved. The seals temperature was 96°·0. Colour of pupil of eye same as that of Ross's seal, metallic green. Stomach empty and only one parasitic nematode. This makes our third seal. *Euphausia* still plentiful amongst honeycombed ice. I shot two blue petrels[2] and missed another bird, like a snowy petrel in appearance, but with darkish bass on its upper wings. Mr Bruce says it is a silver petrel, specimens of which he has already noticed outside the pack edge. Stormy Wilson's, blue and snowy petrels, Cape pigeons and giant petrels, and finners with calves have been seen. Captain saw an albatros[3] asleep on the ice, white head and greyish back. Ross seal, *Ommatophoca rossi*, shot to-day.

Feb. 10th, 60° 05′ S. 32° 10′ W.—Very few birds seen to-day ; Cape pigeons, Wilson's petrels, and nellies, dark colour and white, being the only birds recorded. A snowy petrel was observed to pick a fish out of the water. A Cape pigeon was seen sitting on a piece of ice. Two sea-leopards (*Stenorhynchus leptonyx*), and two examples of *Lobodon* were observed, besides several other seals, too far off to determine. Both *Lobodon* and leopard have been observed in the water as well as on ice ; nearer the South Orkneys they were quite common in the water. Of the three seals already secured only one (Ross) had anything in its stomach. Pirie shot another *Lobodon* on the floe, which was in a state of shedding its coat ; its blubber was 1 in. to 1¼ ins. thick. When Pirie approached the seal, it showed its teeth and uttered a sort of whistling moaning sound, but made no attempt to escape or to attack. Temperature of

---

[1] No doubt *Prion banksi*.

[2] These proved to be specimens of *Prion banksi*.   [3] Very probably a giant petrel.

B

its blood stream was 99°. Eye colour same as yesterday—metallic green, iris brownish.
Mr Bruce saw what was probably a large jelly-fish—orange-coloured, centre about 4 ft.
across. Captain saw two bottle-noses. *Euphausia* still plentiful.

Feb. 11*th*, 60° 03′ S. 32° 31′ W.—Birds more plentiful than yesterday ; Wilson's,
blue, snowy and giant petrels, the latter of both white and dark varieties have been
observed, as well as Cape pigeons. A *Lobodon* was seen on the ice. Two small whales
possibly about 20 ft. long, with head and back greatly resembling those of a finner,
were observed by Mr Bruce and the captain.

Feb. 12*th*, 59° 49′ S. 31° 32′ W.—Wilson's, blue, snowy, silver and giant petrels, as
well as Cape pigeons, were seen during the day. The giant petrel was of the dark
variety. Two Wilson's and one snowy petrel were shot. A large finner and two seals,
one a *Stenorhynchus leptonyx*, were observed by Mr Bruce. Penguins, which we have
not seen since the South Orkneys were out of sight, again appeared, and two ringed
ones were noticed at 10.50 A.M., and others again whilst we were sounding at 11.30 A.M. ;
another batch of four on a piece of ice were seen, but too far off to enable the species
to be determined.

Feb. 13*th*, 59° 43′ S. 30° 44′ W.—Same birds as yesterday. Mr Bruce shot a giant
petrel, a silver petrel and a Cape pigeon. Two external parasites were found on the
silver petrel ; none were found on the other two. The stomach contents of the nelly and
Cape pigeon consisted mostly of *Euphausia*. Some penguins were also seen to-day, but
the species could not be distinguished. The silver petrel and Cape pigeon circled and
crossed the ship ; the former, however, never stays long. Two species of *Euphausia*, one
a large one, transparent and very slightly coloured, an amphipod and a medusoid were
caught in a hand net on the top of submerged ice foot. Two finners and one seal
were observed.

Feb 14*th*, 59° 33′ S. 27° 37′ W.—Birds much more plentiful to-day than yesterday.
Same species seen as yesterday, with the addition of the sooty albatros.[1] Snowy petrels
more scarce, as we have been sailing in open water practically clear of ice. Penguins
were also noticed, both on the ice and in the water. Several finners : no seals.

Feb. 15*th*, 61° 37′ S. 26° 10′ W.—Wilson's, blue, snowy and giant petrels, as well
as a sooty albatros and Cape pigeons seen during day. *Stenorhynchus leptonyx* and
Lobodon carcinophaga also seen on the ice, the latter in a moulting condition. Several
finners. Ringed penguins.

Feb. 16*th*, 62° 52′ S. 25° 00′ W.—Sooty albatros, giant petrel, as well as Wilson's,
blue, snowy, silver and Cape pigeons and antarctic skua. Terns, possibly *Sterna
hirudinacea*,[2] also observed to-day. Plenty of finners all day, especially in the
morning. Several seals were seen on a stream of pack ice about 8 A.M. too far off to
allow one to distinguish the species.

[1] *Phoebetria cornicoides.* This is the species of sooty albatros noted on the succeeding days to 69° 46′ S.
The other species, *P. fuliginosa*, was left behind in 58° S.

[2] Mr W. Eagle Clarke has since determined this Weddell Sea tern as *Sterna macrura*, the Arctic
tern.

Zoological Log of Scottish National Antarctic Expedition.

[Photo by W. S. Bruce.

17. Blue-eyed Shags (*Phalacrocorax atriceps*) on Rudmose Rocks, South Orkneys.

[Photo by W. S. Bruce.

18. Gentoo Penguins (*Pygoscelis papua*) Fishing in Scotia Bay, South Orkneys.

Feb. 17*th*, 64° 18′ S. 23° 09 ′ W.—No penguins to-day. Blue, snowy, and Wilson's petrels recorded to-day, as well as Cape pigeons, one of which was noticed by Mr Bruce as having its secondaries and primaries almost entirely white. *Thalassoeca antarctica*, the antarctic petrel, was seen for the first time to-day. Finners seen in the afternoon, but no seals all day. A copepod and two radiolarians got in yesterday's tow-net.

Feb. 18*th*, 66° 05′ S. 23° 46′ W.—No penguins. Sooty albatros, a nelly, five antarctic petrels, blue, Wilson's and snowy petrels recorded. Most prominent bird to-day was Wilson's petrel. Tern was seen by Mr Bruce.

Feb. 19*th*, 68° 33′ S. 24° 31′ W.—Same terns seen as yesterday; black head, back and side of the neck black, upper surface grey, under surface white. Cape pigeons, snowy, blue, antarctic and Wilson's petrels seen to-day. No finners or seals. Sooty albatros observed. A white-throated penguin was seen about 9.30 P.M., probably the ringed species.

Feb. 20*th*, 69° 39′ S. 22° 58′ W.—Several flocks of snowy petrels seen at different times during the day. Blue, Wilson's and antarctic also recorded, as well as a stray nelly and sooty albatros. Birds, except snowy petrels, not so abundant to-day. Ringed penguins also seen, besides finners and seals, two *Lobodons*, and another, *Stenorhynchus*.

Feb. 21*st*, 69° 46′ S. 19° 10′ W.—Birds, except penguins, more scarce to-day. About thirty penguins *(Pygoscelis adeliæ)* were seen during the day, and one emperor[1] was shot. It weighed 64 lbs, and had a length 51½ inches, with a girth of 36 inches; its body temperature was 100°·2 F. In its stomach cephalopod beaks, fish and three small pebbles (gneiss) were found, and the stomach contents were strongly acid to litmus, those of the rectum slightly acid. Snowy petrels fairly abundant, as well as terns of which there seemed to be two sizes. No Wilson's or blue petrels or Cape pigeons were seen. An antarctic petrel and a nelly or a sooty albatros were recorded. Of whales, finners and bottle-noses have been observed, the former scarce. One *Lobodon* was seen lying on a piece of ice. Two dead fishes, 4 inches to 6 inches long, were seen lying on a piece of ice, probably disgorged by a petrel. *Euphausia* has not been seen amongst the pancake ice which is now forming.

Feb. 22*nd*, 70° 21′ S. 17° 00′ W.—About two dozen snowy petrels and only one Wilson's recorded to-day. Abundant adelia penguins and some emperors; a specimen of the latter was captured. Many seals (*Lobodon*) mostly white in colour were observed lying on pieces of ice. The captain heard a finner blowing about 6 P.M.

Feb. 23*rd*, 69° 57′ S. 16° 53′ W.—A few snowy petrels, two antarctic petrels, and black-throated (adelia) penguins in considerable numbers. No finners. Three seals (*Lobodon*) on one piece of ice and a fourth on another piece make up the total number of beasts seen to-day. Three black-throated penguins were captured this evening; their temperature was taken (by rectum), 102° F. These were adult birds, showing moulting feathers which were white at the base, brownish at the apex, and black at the tips.

---

[1] *Aptenodytes forsteri.*

The new coat of feathers was of a steely-blue and bluey-black colour. These are heavier birds than the ringed or antarctic penguins.

Feb. 24th, 69° 52′ S. 17° 22′ W.—One antarctic and a few snowy petrels seen. Black-throated penguins abundant. About a dozen seals were observed during the day, including several *Lobodon carcinophaga.* Two black-throated penguins were captured this evening, one by Mr Bruce, the other by myself; the former showed moulting feathers only on the crown of its head ; the latter had none. Of four others two had their new coats, and two were in the same condition as yesterday's birds. Temperature of one penguin by rectum was 103°·4 F.

Feb 25th, 69° 44′ S. 18° 02′ W.—Snowy petrels observed several times during the day, and only one antarctic petrel. Black-throated penguins were in abundance. Two grampuses and several seals were seen. Several penguins were caught. These penguins have not yet been observed leaping out of the water like porpoises, in the manner of the ringed species in the vicinity of the South Orkneys. Radiolarians and copepods plentiful in tow-net.

Feb. 26th, 69° 36′ S. 20° 20′ W.—Snowy petrels and black-throated penguins are the only birds that have been seen to-day. A "spout" of a whale was seen, but no other animals have been observed.

Feb. 27th, 69° 32′ S. 24° 00′ W.—Birds far more numerous to-day. Flocks of snowy petrels were constantly flying about the ship, while several flocks of antarctic petrels were about in the evening, and a few Wilson's petrels were observed at noon. Black-throated penguins were also seen during the day sitting on pieces of ice. Several seals (*Lobodon*) were also recorded. The captain saw a grampus.

Feb. 28th, 69° 22′ S. 26° 36′ W.—To-day in addition to yesterday's birds we saw several terns, two Wilson's petrels and one nelly. Pirie shot two snowy petrels and one tern. Several seals (*Lobodon carcinophaga*) were observed, as well as a few grampuses. Found a small medusoid in a sample of water taken yesterday for analysis. The Hensen quantitative plankton net was lowered to a depth of 200 fathoms, and a polychaete worm, numerous copepods and radiolarians, besides examples of *Sagitta* were obtained in it.

March 1st, 69° 03′ S. 28° 2′ W.—Several hundreds of penguins (adelia) were seen during the day ; snowy petrels numerous, a few antarctic petrels and one or two Wilson's, as well as terns. Several seals (*Lobodon*) were recorded lying on pieces of ice. Grampuses also numerous.

March 2nd, 68° 40′ S. 30° 18′ W.—A good many snowy petrels, a few antarctic and Wilson's petrels and terns. One antarctic petrel was shot by Walker. No penguins seen till this evening when one was observed, but I could not make out whether it was an emperor ; possibly a new species. I shot at it but failed to secure it. *Sagitta* and *Globigerina buloides* and copepods in the tow-net.

March 3rd, 68° 35′ S. 31° 56′ W.—Snowy petrels numerous ; terns and antarctic petrels frequently seen. Pirie shot a seal, a very old male *Lobodon* ; it was fastened to

Zoological Log of Scottish National Antarctic Expedition.

[Photo by W. S. Bruce.

19. Gentoo Penguins (*Pygoscelis papua*) fishing in Scotia Bay, South Orkneys. Tail up!

[Photo by W. S. Bruce.

20. Blue-eyed Shags (*Phalacrocorax atriceps*) nesting on Shag Rock, opposite Point Thomson.

[Photo by W. S. Bruce.

21. MacDougall and a Friendly Blue-eyed Shag.

[Photo by W. S. Bruce.

22. Blue-eyed Shag, Nest, and Egg.

a line and lowered down as bait for some three grampuses, which were quite close to it ; they, however, did not take the bait, but we succeeded in getting a good view of them, and the opportunity was taken by the artist to get their form and colour. Cuthbertson shot two terns. Two or three species were among the host of *Euphausia* in the seal's stomach. The seal had a recent scar between the angle of the mouth and the angle of the lower jaw, about 4 inches long, which was beginning to heal up. Underneath the scar on the outer surface of the lower jaw there was an area of acute periostitis, part of the bone being separated as a sequestrum. Several of the teeth were decayed, and all the teeth showed that the animal was old. The coat was entirely new, with the exception of two bands on either side of the middle line of the abdomen where the old yellowish coat was seen. This new coat was of a paler grey than those other *Lobodons* we have previously captured and seen, and the markings were not so distinct. The eyes appeared to be more prominent, and the forehead broader and flatter. The toe-nails of all the *Lobodons* are complete, five on each flipper. A siphonophore tentacle was caught on the sounding wire.

March 4th, 68° 22′ S. 32° 35′ W.—Snowy petrels very numerous. Terns and antarctic petrels not so plentiful as yesterday. Saw two seals swimming and some grampuses. The two seals seemed to be *Lobodon* from the appearance of their heads.

March 5th, 68° 11′ S. 34° 17′ W.—Snowy petrels and terns in great numbers and a few antarctic petrels. A few grampuses were seen, one of them had its dorsal fin broken. The Monagasque trawl was lowered in 1280 fathoms. The dynomometer registered a maximum strain of 1½ tons. This was a purely experimental lowering not intended to reach the bottom. Three or four species of animals were secured including *Sagitta*, *Doliolum*, a medusoid and another coelenterate. Sea slightly phosphorescent at 9.45 P.M.

March 6th, 67° 39′ S. 36° 10′ W.—Snowy petrels, and a good many terns, one nelly and a few antarctic petrels. Captain saw a school of grampuses. Over 100 penguins were seen during the day ; some of them were black-throated, the others could not be made out. The trawl was lowered away with 1850 fathoms of wire rope, but owing to an accident it had to be hauled up again before reaching bottom (2500 fathoms). Maximum pressure 2 tons 8 cwts. Nevertheless several animals were secured, two species of nemerteans, specimens of *Sagitta*, two pterpods, a large ostracod, besides some unknown species.

March 7th, 67° 33′ S. 36° 35′ W.—Snowy petrels still numerous ; terns, one nelly and black-throated penguins make up the list of birds seen to-day. Lowered away trawl to 2500 fathoms bottom and dragged for three-quarters of an hour, securing one fish,[1] one gasteropod, three lamellibranchs, two fragments of small crustaceans, four or five species of holothurians, a flat sea-urchin, two spines of a sea-urchin, stalked crinoids, brittle stars, and two species of alcyonaria, a sponge and many spicules, two or

---

[1] *Neobythites Brucei*, sp. nov.

three species of bryozoa, worm tubes and several other animals including three species of foraminifers.

March 8th, 67° 22' S. 37° 36' W.—Snowy petrels and adelia penguins numerous ; a nelly, antarctic petrels ; also one seal.

March 9th, 67° 10' S. 39° 00' W.—Birds not so numerous to-day ; terns, snowy petrels, antarctic petrels and penguins. An emperor penguin was shot to-day by MacDougall. Several seals were seen lying in the water.

March 10th, 66° 40' S. 40° 35' W.—Two adelia penguins were caught this morning by the cooks and some others were seen in the evening. Snowy and antarctic petrels and terns were also seen. Shot a bird in the evening, like a Cape hen, only smaller, probably M'Cormick's skua.[1] Lowered away trawl this morning to 2425 fathoms ; paid out 3000 fathoms of wire rope. Secured a rich haul with very little mud. The contents of the haul include two species of sea-urchins, two species of ophiuroids, two species of holothurians, a cepholopod, a polychaete, *Doliolum* and two species of forams.

March 11th, 66° 22' S. 42° 20' W.—Several antarctic and snowy petrels, about 20 skuas, probably of the same species as the one shot yesterday, besides a nelly, terns, Wilson's and blue petrels[2] and a few adelia penguins comprise the list of birds seen to-day. Wilson's and blue petrels we have not seen for some time. A seal was seen this morning.

March 12th, 65° 29' S. 44° 06' W.—Snowy petrels abundant and a few antarctic petrels were seen as well as a nelly. Captain saw bottle-noses twice. The "Scotia" closing net was lowered to 100 and 500 fathoms respectively ; a small catch. The "tak' a' net" was lowered, but unfortunately a kink occured on the wire and the net was lost.

March 13th, 64° 48' S. 44° 26' W.—A few snowy petrels and penguins are the only birds seen to-day. Could not make out the species of the penguins, but probably black-throated. Grampuses and seals observed. Davidson saw a sea-leopard and I saw a seal after sunset, probably a *Lobodon*. Lowered away trawl to bottom in 2485 fathoms, blue mud ; paid out 3000 fathoms of wire. Time from 10.15 A.M. to 5.15 P.M. Secured a rich haul, including two species of medusoids, two species of siliceous sponges, one of them stalked, a stalked crinoid, ten specimens of ophiuroids quite intact, a crustacean probably a schizopod, a broken lamellibranch, probably a *Pecten* or allied to it, etc. Mr Bruce secured a polychaete on the wire from between the surface and 500 fathoms. *Dentalium, Serpula* and *Nodosaria* also figure in the catch.

March 14th, 64° 30' S. 43° 45' W.—Adelia penguins and snowy petrels are the only birds recorded to-day and very few of the latter. One *Lobodon*, a finner whose "blast" was seen and several seals complete the list of animals seen to-day.

March 15th, 64° 12' S. 42° 15' W.—Snowy petrels abundant ; several adelia penguins, one antarctic petrel, four terns and two nellies were seen during the day.

[1] One of the two specimens of *Megalestris maccormicki* obtained by the Expedition.
[2] *Halobœna cœrulea* in all probability.

Zoological Log of Scottish National Antarctic Expedition.

[Photo by W. S. Bruce.

23. Black-throated Penguins (*Pygoscalis adeliæ*) on Point Martin, South Orkneys. A Fight!

[Photo by W. S. Bruce.

24. Black-throated Penguins on Graptolite Island, South Orkneys. Running the Gauntlet!

[Photo by W. S. Bruce.

25.

[Photo by J. H. H. Pirie.

26.

[Photo by W. S. Bruce.

27.

Emperor Penguins (*Antenodytes forsteri*). Height fully 3 feet. Weight about 70 to 80 lbs.

Mr Bruce saw a seal in the forenoon, but could not distinguish the species. Fragments of siphonophore tentacles caught on sounding wire.

March 16th, 63° 51′ S. 40° 50′ W.—A great bird day; Cape pigeons, Wilson's petrels and silver petrels have been seen to-day, all of which birds have not been recorded for a long time. Antarctic petrels fairly common; adelia penguins and snowy petrels abundant and some terns. Grampuses have been seen by the captain. Lowered away trawl in 2550 fathoms; 3000 fathoms of rope out; did not, however, actually touch bottom, so only got a few beasts, including a fish (deep sea) and medusoids (three species).

March 17th, 63° 08′ S. 42° 30′ W.—Another great bird day; Cape pigeons, snowy, silver, Wilson's, giant and blue petrels seen during day. The blue petrel has not been seen for some considerable time. Mr Bruce saw some 20 or 30 penguins seated on a iceberg 40 or 50 feet high; they must have jumped four to five feet out of the water to have got on to the berg. Terns were also seen flying about. Saw a sea-leopard *(Stenorhynchus leptonyx)* lying on a piece of ice.

March 18th, 62° 10′ S. 41° 20′ W.—Same birds as yesterday with the exception of penguins. Lowered away trawl in 1775 fathoms with about 2300 to 2400 fathoms of wire rope; contents included about 36 species. Two species of fish, two species of gasteropods and two of lamellibranchs, two species of pycnogons, a *Caprella* and an amphipod, a few species of chaetopods, a species of barnacle, one or two species of bryozoa, seven or eight of asteroids, two of crinoids, two of echinoids represented only by spines, one holothurian, a species of alcyonaria, two species of sponge and four of foraminifers.

March 19th, 61° 22′ S. 42° 05′ W.—Snowy and silver petrels abundant; a flock of Wilson's petrels were observed by the captain sitting on the water. Cape pigeons and blue petrels fairly common, also terns. Saw some white-throated penguins, probably antarctic, sitting on a piece of ice. One finner and seals, a *Lobodon* and a *Stenorhynchus*, have also been seen.

March 20th, 61° 05′ S. 43° 20′ W.—Snowy petrels and an albatros *(Diomedea exulans)* were the only birds seen to-day. Misty and overcast all day.

March 21st, Leathwaite Strait, South Orkneys.—Many Cape pigeons, silver and Wilson's petrels, several sooty albatroses and nellies, one skua, sheathbills, antarctic and snowy petrels, shags and ringed penguins. Several finners also recorded for to-day.

March 22nd, Between Saddle Island and Cape Bennett, South Orkneys.—Cape pigeons, nellies, sheathbills, skuas, antarctic, Wilson's, snowy and silver petrels and finners have been seen to-day.

March 23rd, Leathwaite Strait, South Orkneys.—In the morning whilst out at sea several snowy, silver, Wilson's and antarctic petrels seen. Whilst out in the boat looking for Spence Harbour, saw several shags, nellies, Cape hens, skuas, gulls, terns, sheathbills, ringed penguins and the gentoo penguin *(Pygoscelis papua)*. Specimens were secured of the last two named birds and a young black-backed gull. In the evening whilst in Ellisen Harbour saw two Weddell seals, one of which was very tame and allowed us without concern to stroke him. Mr Bruce saw a ctenophore about three or four inches long in Spence Harbour, and a star-fish was seen. Grampuses and finners were also sighted.

March 24th, Off the South Orkneys, 61° 14′ S. 44° 50′ W.—Ringed penguins, snowy petrels, a sheathbill and Wilson's petrels were seen to-day, as well as several seals, too far off to distinguish the species.

March 25th, Off Murray Islands, South Orkneys.—Very few birds seen till we approached the land from which we had been blown some 30 miles during the night. Only one or two silver, one Wilson's and a brace of snowy petrels were noticed when far away from land. Hundreds of shags, penguins, both antarctic and gentoo, black-backed gulls, nellies, skuas and terns were met with when we were out in the boat near land. Mr Bruce saw a sea-leopard before breakfast, and a Weddell seal was observed at 10 o'clock. A specimen of the latter, a female, was secured later on, shot in Buchan Bay. A compound ascidian was obtained after we had lowered the boat, and Brown got a *Patella* and some amphipods from a rock in Buchan Bay, and saw a star-fish and a *Doliolum.* Bryozoa were got in the Lucas sounding gripper, whilst sounding in 40 and 18 fathoms, and also a sponge in 40 fathoms. Pirie shot an adult black-backed gull. Anchored at night in Scotia Bay.

March 26th, Scotia Bay, South Orkneys,[1] 60° 43′ S. 44° 38′ W.—Pirie caught a nelly asleep on the ice; MacDougall shot a skua and a sheathbill. The temperature of the latter was 107°·3 F. Flocks of shags, several snowy petrels and skuas, sheathbills and penguins, gentoo and antarctic, were seen. Pirie and Ross saw several Weddell seals of different sizes, some large and some small. In the trap were two large isopods,[2] two small pycnogons and a large pycnogon of a bright orange colour with ten legs,[3] three gasteropods and a number of amphipods[4] resembling *Onesimus,* besides two or three other species. The trap was lowered to about 12 fathoms. Mr Bruce secured along the shore many amphipods and limpets, besides two acarinids and some collembolids; one of the acarinids was new, the rest of them the same as were obtained on Saddle Island. Whilst on shore we collected some whales ribs and two vertebræ.

March 27th.—Mr Bruce saw some snowy petrels about 500 feet up the cliffs. The usual South Orkney birds were seen during the day. The Bay being free of ice the trap was hauled up and we secured two large fish like a *Notothenia,*[5] a bryozoon, a polychaete, several gasteropods and a great number of amphipods.

March 28th.—Hauled up net this morning and secured several very interesting specimens. Fishes like *Notothenia,* two compound ascidians, many pycnogons, some isopods, a whole host of amphipods, young as well as adult, numerous gasteropods, one species of lamellibranch and star-fishes. A small fish like a haddock was found

---

[1] The *Scotia* remained here in winter quarters until liberated on Nov. 24th.   [2] *Glyptonotus acutus.*
[3] *Decalopoda australis.* The small pycnogons were *Chaetonymphon orcadense* and *Nymphon orcadense,* both new species.   [4] Probably *Orchomenopsis rossi.*   [5] *Notothenia coriiceps.*

Scot. Nat. Ant. Exp. (Vol. iv., Part i.).

PLATE X.

Zoological Log of Scottish National Antarctic Expedition.

[Photo by W. S. Bruce.

28. Weddell Seal (*Leptonychotes weddelli*) off Coats Land.

[Photo by W. S. Bruce.

29. Weddell Seals on Mossman Peninsula, Scotia Bay.

[Photo by W. S. Bruce.

30. Finner Whale (*Balænoptera sp. ?*).

[Photo by W. S. Bruce.

31. Two Finner Whales.

inside one of the other fishes stomachs. The cooks caught a large stout nemertean[1] on a line; after the worm had been brought up it ejected the inch long bait and hook. Skuas, paddies, gentoo and antarctic penguins, snowy petrels and gulls were seen during the day.

March 29th.—Gentoo and antarctic penguins, nellies and a gull have been recorded to-day.

March 30th and 31st.—Gentoo and antarctic penguins, nellies, sheathbills and skuas have been seen during these two days, besides several Weddell seals.

April 1st.—Paddies around the ship eating refuse.

April 2nd.—Gentoo and antarctic penguins, nellies, sheathbills, skuas, three shags and one gull (young *Larus dominicanus*) were seen to-day. Since the harbour has been covered with ice, very few shags have been observed. A Weddell seal was clubbed by some of the men, and an embryo was secured from it. Some fish and a star-fish were caught on the line by the cooks. Pirie shot two nellies near the carcase of a seal.

April 3rd.—Several batches of penguins, about 50 to 200 in each batch, were seen going north, and then coming back again. They march in single file, and when chased they move quite as quick as a man, and go up very steep places. They have been seen in places about 400 feet above sea level.

April 4th.—Sheathbills, skuas, nellies, young and old gulls (*Larus dominicanus*), and both species of penguins have been recorded to-day. The sheathbills are always about the ship picking up refuse, and are quite tame; on shore also they are always about the tent. Several seals have been seen.

April 5th.—Sheathbills, nellies, skuas, gulls and a few gentoo penguins comprise the list of birds seen to-day. In the afternoon there was not a single penguin to be seen on the north side of Scotia Bay. Saw one Weddell seal asleep on the ice.

April 6th.—The same birds as yesterday. The gulls both young and old were in greater force than yesterday. Heard several penguins last night.

April 7th.—Sheathbills, snowy petrels, shags, skuas, nellies, gulls, adult and young, and a few gentoo penguins were seen to-day. Specimens of a shag and two snowy petrels were secured. In the afternoon lowered the small dredge[2] (about 11 to 12 fathoms bottom) in an open lane and secured several specimens.

April 8th.—The same birds seen as yesterday. A considerable number of penguins were observed going along the foot of the eastern glacier. A ringed penguin was seen by Mossman among a flock of gentoos. Two skuas and a nelly were shot to-day. Weddell seals were seen both yesterday and to-day; one came up several times in an open lane whilst we were dredging. Lowered middle-sized dredge to-day in same place as yesterday; the depth there is $9\frac{1}{2}$ fathoms, increasing to $10\frac{1}{4}$ fathoms towards the ship.

April 9th.—Early in the morning Pirie and I went over to Uruguay Cove.

---

[1] This animal, a species of *Euborlasia*, was very common, and is frequently referred to throughout the winter as the "large nemertean."

[2] This dredge was the one used throughout the winter. The dimensions of its mouth were 6″ by $2\frac{1}{2}$ feet.

C

We shot a skua, and we saw several others, as well as gulls, snowy petrels, nellies, sheathbills, Cape pigeons and an immense flock of shags flying northwards in more or less V-shaped groups. After breakfast we went along the south-west shore to a big gentoo rookery at Point Martin, where we saw a few ringed penguins and three black-throated ones among them, two of which latter were secured. Mr Bruce brought a young adelia (throat quite white) and two gentoos from the west shore. Sheathbills still continue tame and hop about, sometimes on one leg, picking up refuse. Had middle-sized dredge[1] out this morning in the same place. Our catch for the three days includes two species of fish, a large soft spiny tunicate, several specimens of lamellibranchs, a few gasteropods, including one large limpet, brachiopods, pycnogons, three or four species of crustaceans, large nemerteans, several specimens of "worms," about four or five species of star-fish, several sea-urchins, about three species of holothurians and several species of sponges. Cuthbertson painted a small fish, a polychaete, a star-fish, a holothurian, a sponge and the eye and feet of a young adelia.

April 10*th.*—Had a dredge down again in the same place and secured several species of molluscs, pycnogons, isopods, and some amphipods, besides a polychaete and three or four other species of "worms," some large nemerteans, star-fishes and several sponges. The same kind of birds were observed as yesterday, with the exception of Cape pigeons. Shags were seen in flight to-day over the open water in Jessie Bay. A nelly was shot and a male Weddell seal was secured this morning; the contents of its stomach consisted of fish, fish bones and otocysts, and molluscs. Ribbon worms were also found in its stomach. After lunch visited a batch of seals (eleven in number, all Weddells) which were lying on the ice a few hundred yards from the ship. They allowed us to get quite close, and would not budge until we forced them to do so by striking them hard with a stick, when they would wriggle away until out of breath, then turn on their backs, raise their heads and look at us sleepily. Their mode of progression on ice is by hunching their backs, then stretching as far forward as possible, and bringing their hind flippers up to repeat the movement.

April 11*th.*—A trap lowered yesterday afternoon down a seal hole some distance away from the ship was hauled up twice to-day; nothing but fish secured in it. The dredge to-day brought up star-fishes, the usual molluscs, worms and crustaceans. Not so many birds to-day, probably on account of the weather which was misty and mild.

April 12*th.*—A new species of isopod,[2] two small fish, brittle stars, sea-urchins and numerous large nemerteans were got in the dredge to-day. Yesterday and to-day were rather misty days, and only penguins, paddies, skuas, snowy petrels and Cape pigeons were seen. From the trap some ten fishes, some star-fishes and two isopods were collected. A skua was shot yesterday and another one to-day.

April 14*th.*—Only one fish and a pycnogon were obtained in the trap. From the

---

[1] The dredge was hauled in the same place twice each day until October, and though on identically the same ground continued to bring up not only an abundance of specimens, but, from time to time, new species.
[2] *Glyptonotus acutus.*

dredge an interesting specimen of a compound ascidian, which was obviously torn up from a fixed base, was secured—besides a fish, a new isopod (same as yesterday—probably the young form of the big isopod which we have already secured), pycnogons, lamellibranchs and gasteropods, etc. Snowy petrels, young and adult gulls, sheath-bills, nellies and some penguins make up the list of birds seen to-day. Came across about thirty adelias on the floe, and secured two specimens, one an adult with black throat complete, the other just beginning to show signs of a black throat. The temperature of the adult was 105°·5, of the other 104°·6 F.

April 15th.—The dredge to-day brought up a small fish, two specimens of tunicates, limpets and another gasteropod, pycnogons, a big isopod, a large amphipod, two sea-urchins, several star-fish, two ophiuroids, large nemerteans, polychaetes, a new sponge, of which a careful painting has been made, and several other sponges. The trap contained five fish, one star-fish and a large isopod. A gentoo and an adelia penguin as well as a snowy petrel were shot to-day, the former two for skeletons. Paddies, snowy petrels, Cape pigeons, nellies, skuas and penguins were seen to-day, besides hundreds of shags, and young and old gulls. The ringed penguins have been very scarce since our first week here, and only solitary ones among a batch of gentoos are now met with.

April 16th.—From the dredge the following animals were secured : fish, tunicates, molluscs, pycnogons, amphipods, " worms," star-fish, ophiuroids, and last, but not least, a new sea-anemone. Fishes (the biggest measured 16 ins., and weighed 1 lb. 10 ozs.), isopods and star-fishes were got in the trap. A line was baited and shot in open sea to the south, off Point Martin, and three fishes[1] (*Notothenia*) and three star-fishes were caught : it was only down for a short time or the catch would have been larger. In the afternoon Pirie and Brown dredged and fished Uruguay Cove, but without success, and the dredge only brought up mud. The usual birds seen to-day. Mr Bruce also saw some young skuas which were mottled.

April 17th.—A new nudibranch was caught in the dredge, besides the other usual animals. Only a star-fish was secured in the small trap, which was changed to the west side of the bay. The big trap was also lowered this afternoon in a hole about 200 yards south-west of the ship in 15 fathoms. Several seals have been seen for the past three days. Usual birds seen, and two Cape pigeons secured.

April 18th.—Dredge contained a small fish, tunicates, limpets and other gasteropods including a shell resembling *Mya truncata*, a large red amphipod, some isopods, pycnogons, cushion-stars, star-fishes, sea-urchins, including a young one, 1 in. in diameter, and of the same colour as the adult, several holothurians, including a new one, which the artist has carefully painted, polychaetes, large nemerteans and the usual bryozoa and sponges. Small trap contained a star-fish.

April 19th.—Large trap only contained one big fish weighing 2 lbs. 14 ozs., and measuring 17½ ins., and ten gasteropods. A line was shot yesterday afternoon, and

---

[1] *Notothenia coriiceps.* This abundant species was by far the commonest one in Scotia Bay, and was caught almost daily.

hauled up this morning, with fishes like *Notothenia* on it. The big trap contained two pin-cushion star-fishes, two pycnogons, a few isopods and some gasteropods. Birds and seals plentiful; of the former, nellies, one a white one, snowy petrels, Cape pigeons, sheathbills, black-backed gulls, young and adult, skuas and numerous shags. Mr Bruce saw a white bird like a black-backed gull, possibly an albino gull. Several birds were shot.

April 20th.—Very poor dredge to-day, consisting of a tunicate, a few pycnogons, cushion-stars, a sea-urchin, holothurians and bits of sponges. The big trap yielded five fish, pycnogons, amphipods galore, more than twelve gasteropods and cushion-stars. The small trap near the shore in 2 fathoms brought up only one star-fish. A line was shot this morning, and taken up at 4 P.M. with six fish; it was set again. A big seal, evidently disturbed in feasting, came up when the line was being hauled in. The same birds as yesterday. We got about six nellies for skeleton purposes. Many ringed penguins were observed at the waters edge.

April 21st.—From the dredge two beautiful pycnogons[1] were secured in the act of copulation; a careful drawing and painting was made; also a new fish, and the usual other animals. From the large trap some fish were secured, as well as isopods, amphipods, gasteropods and cushion-stars. The line and small trap yielded only two fish and some star-fish; sheathbills, snowy petrels, shags, skuas and nellies quite plentiful. A flock of Cape pigeons was observed flying north. Penguins very scarce.

April 22nd.—In the dredge were a tunicate, pycnogons, isopods, a polychaete, the usual molluscs, bryozoa, cushion- and star-fishes, and sponges, but no fish. Large trap contained gasteropods, amphipods, isopods, " worms," cushion- and star-fishes. Only one fish was on the line, and the small trap contained no beasts. A drove of penguins was seen on Point Davis glacier. Gulls, skuas, snowy petrels, paddies and nellies also observed.

April 23rd.—To-day's catch the same as yesterday's, very poor indeed. The same applies to the large trap, the position of which was changed to-day. Same kind of birds observed to-day as yesterday. Seals were also seen.

April 24th.—The dredge was not hauled nor the traps examined to-day. Only two gulls were seen.

April 25th.—The catch in the dredge was very poor to-day; only some pycnogons and star-fishes. The trap was lowered yesterday in 25 fathoms, stony bottom, and, on examination to-day, six large fish (of *Notothenia* type), a large quantity of amphipods and six gasteropods were found. Birds very scarce; sheathbills and some nellies seen.

April 26th.—Shags seen by Mr Bruce; a few seals observed.

April 27th.—The dredge contained one small fish, some small gasteropods, small pycnogons, and one large pycnogon of a dark crimson colour, with black head and claws, some isopods, several amphipods, a new planarian worm, several chaetopods, and other " worms," the usual echinoderms, excepting crinoids, and sponges. The trap contained three fish (*Notothenia*), another small one, a big gasteropod, amphipods galore,

[1] *Decalopoda australis.*

Zoological Log of Scottish National Antarctic Expedition.

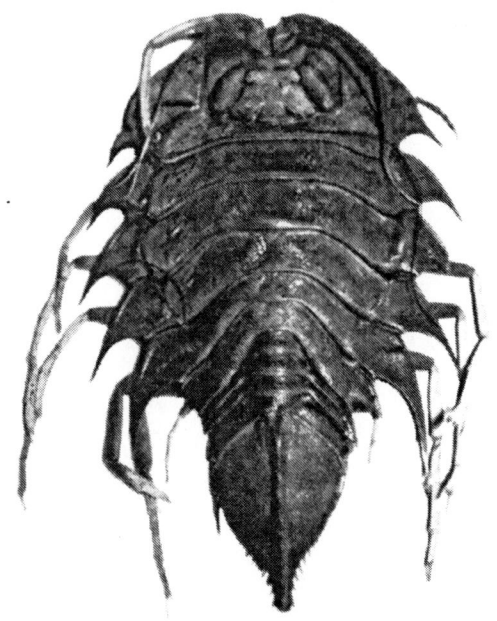

[*Photo by W. S. Bruce.*

[*Photo by W. S. Bruce.*

32. A Shallow Water Antarctic Isopod (*Glyptonotus antarcticus*), taken in Scotia Bay, 10 to 20 fathoms. (⅓ natural size.)

33. A New Species of Deep Water Antarctic Isopod (*Scrolis meridionalis*), taken near Coats Land in 1410 fathoms, lat. 71° 22′ S., long. 16° 34′ W. (1¼ natural size.)

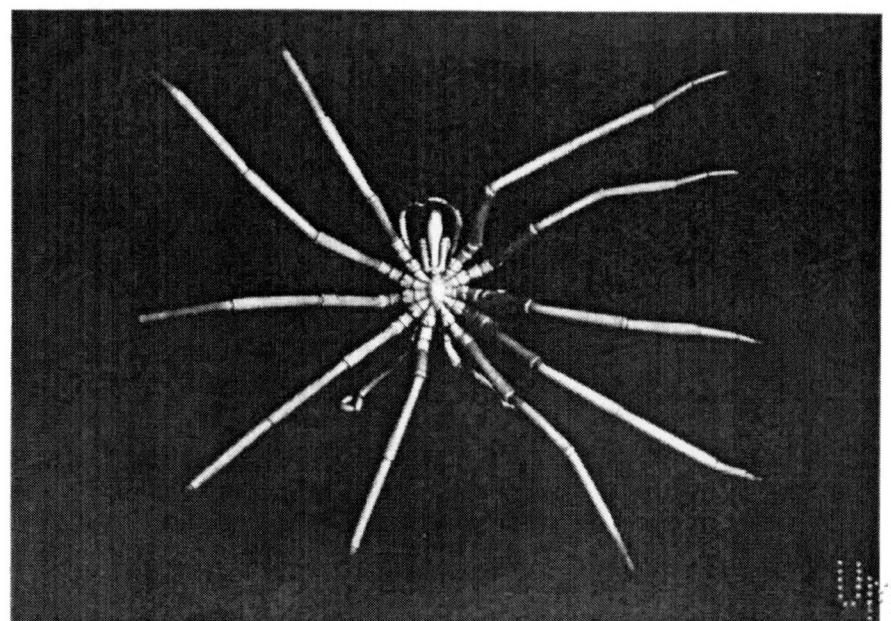

[*Photo by T. C. Day.*

34. A Long-lost Ten-legged Sea Spider (*Decalopoda australis*) rediscovered by the "Scotia" Naturalists. (⅔ natural size.)

and a new species of cushion-star, colour salmon, adorned with crimson patches. There were signs of seals having being near the trap. Several snowy petrels, sheathbills, gulls, young and adult, and a nelly seen to-day. Penguins have not been seen for a day or two. Several seals were seen again to-day.

April 28th.—The first time the dredge was hauled up it had only one large nemertean in it; the second time it contained five pycnogons, a small isopod and a cushion-star. The trap contained nil. Two skuas, snowy petrels, sheathbills and several hundred penguins, mostly gentoos, were observed; also some seals. Pirie made the following remarks about the penguins mode of progression. When marching over hard surface they maintain an upright position, marching in column of route, but whenever they come to soft snow they assume the prone position, and propel themselves by means of their hind legs; ascending a slope or being chased on the level or elsewhere they bring their flippers into play, using them either alternately or synchronously; when descending from any height they toboggan.

April 29th.—The contents of the dredge were some chitons, a few pycnogons, and amphipods, one isopod, a few polychaetes, some sea-urchins and star-fishes. The trap contained one fish (*Notothenia*), some buckies and amphipods. Very poor catch, but a little better than yesterday. A few penguins, snowy petrels and the usual paddies were seen. Where the trap is lowered, a seal comes every morning to have a look at its being hauled up; he saves himself the work of making a hole of his own by utilising this one.

April 30th.—The dredge contained some small molluscs, some pycnogons, isopods and amphipods, various "worms," two holothurians, star-fishes, sea-urchins and feather-stars, bryozoa and sponges. None of the species were new except one "worm." In the trap were one large fish, star-fish, some gasteropods, amphipods and pycnogons. Very few birds to-day, only some penguins, snowy petrels and paddies.

May 1st.—The dredge contained chitons and small gasteropods, isopods and pycnogons, polychaetes and several other "worms," worm tubes, one sea-urchin, several star-fishes, one holothurian and a sponge. The trap (21 fathoms) contained two small isopods, amphipods galore and one red pycnogon, besides two cushion-stars. A dozen gentoo penguins, the ubiquitous paddies and some snowy petrels were seen to-day.

May 2nd.—In the dredge were the usual molluscs and crustaceans, "worms" and worm-tubes, several sea-urchins, star-fishes, brittle-stars and holothurians. In the trap were seven fishes and two star-fishes. Birds are scarce; even the paddies are represented by few individuals; snowy petrels and one gull were also seen.

May 4th.—The contents of the dredge were the usual molluscs, crustaceans, "worms," star-fishes, holothurians and sponges. In the trap were twenty fish, weighing 31 lbs. 1 oz.; the biggest one, a female, weighed 4 lbs. 6 ozs.; there were also two star-fishes. The first haul of the dredge for the last week or so has been very poor and sometimes nil, the second haul being the more productive. The trap contained a record catch to-day. About a dozen paddies, two or three snowy petrels, two nellies and four black-backed gulls were seen to-day.

May 5th.—The dredge contained the usual molluscs, crustaceans, "worms," star-fishes, several holothurians and several sponges. The trap contained seven fish, five female and two male, total weight 7 lbs. 10 ozs., the usual amphipods and several star-fishes. The fish contained a nematode and other "ova-like" parasitic forms, which have been preserved. A considerable number of snowy petrels were seen on ridge of Mossman Peninsula between Scotia Bay and Wilton Bay at about 490 feet. One black-backed gull and one nelly besides several paddies were also observed.

May 6th.—Two hauls of the dredge were taken as usual but the catch was small, except for some four or five holothurians, pycnogons, limpets, a few species of sponge, five star-fish, a polychaete, a large nemertean and a tunicate. The trap contained nothing but amphipods. The number of species of birds is rapidly diminishing, only paddies and snowy petrels being seen to-day. One paddy came on board of its own accord and found its way into the 'tween deck laboratory in search of food, but other-wise these birds seem hardly so tame as they were at first; probably they have been frightened by the dogs chasing them.

May 7th.—Quite a number of frozen-over seal holes were seen in Jessie Bay. A specimen of the same holothurian as was obtained on the 10th April was caught in the dredge, also two specimens of the large scarlet pycnogon[1] (caught on April 27th and figured on the 21st). The two specimens were in the act of copulation as before, and, when separated in the laboratory on two occasions, again tried to copulate. The one (as in the specimen of April 27th) was slightly darker than the other, and it was probably the female, but this was not positively observed. In addition, smaller pycnogons, amphipods, cushion-stars, a sea-urchin, another holothurian, several polychaetes and a small lamellibranch were also contained in the catch. Nothing was caught in the trap to-day. The birds seen were paddies and snowy petrels, two shags flying north, a nelly over Jessie Bay, and three gulls in the same place, while during the afternoon a solitary gentoo penguin came up from the south, crossed The Beach and moved towards Saddle Island over Jessie Bay. Two paddies are now on board, one came of its own accord, the other was found by Mr Bruce on the ice partly frozen. Both have become quite tame. A paddy was also observed bathing in the water at the edge of Uruguay Cove to-day.

An experiment was begun yesterday with a view of finding out the power of animals to resist freezing. Two living cushion-stars and a sea-urchin were frozen in salt water in a basin on deck for 24 hours and then thawed out gradually, but all were dead. The thawing was however not very satisfactory and was possibly too fast; further experiments are being made.

May 8th.—Both hauls of the dredge were poor, and the catch consisted of cushion-stars, star-fish, pycnogons, a holothurian, some large nemerteans, bryozoa and small

[1] *Decalopoda australis.*

crustaceans. The trap had seven fish; two big females weighing 3 lbs. 10 ozs., and 3 lbs. 7 ozs. respectively, and full of almost mature ova, and five small males. Total weight of the seven fish was 12 lbs. 8 ozs., average 1 lb. 12½ ozs. The cushion-star frozen for twelve hours and thawed out was again dead; as in yesterday's specimens the tube feet were fully expanded, and the tip of one arm was turned back.

Snowy petrels, paddies, and a black-backed gull were seen about the ship and The Beach, while in Jessie Bay two Cape pigeons and a nelly were seen. Snowy petrels were particularly abundant at one cliff, and there were probably about 100 there with two Cape pigeons among them. The "galley" paddy again came aboard as well as another one. Along Pirie Peninsula, Pirie and I saw two Weddell seals lying on the ice. They were less good-natured and easy-going than the average Weddell, and resented our playing with them. Weddell seals were also seen in Scotia Bay by Mr Bruce.

May 9th.—The dredge contained a small silver and orange-coloured fish, tunicates, sea-urchins, cushion-stars and other star-fish, pycnogons, including a big scarlet one, a large polychaete and the usual bryozoa, etc. The trap contained eight fish, weight 8 lbs; the biggest weighed 1 lb. 11 ozs., measured 14·8 ins. in length, and was a female. Of the remaining seven two were males, four females and one, which was frozen alive, was not determined. There was also one buckie in the trap—these, which were at first so commonly caught in the trap, are now becoming extremely rare.

In addition to the paddies and snowy petrels, a black-backed gull was seen by Ramsay. The "galley" paddy again came on board. The fish put out to freeze yesterday is only partly frozen as the temperature was not low enough to complete the process, but it was dead. Another was put out to freeze to-day, but the temperature was too high.

May 10th.—The dredge was not lowered nor the trap examined to-day. Paddies and snowy petrels were seen by Mr Bruce. I saw a bird which was either a black-backed gull or a nelly; it was too dark to distinguish which.

May 11th.—On account of the south-east gale with driving snow, no dredge was taken or trap examined. Paddies were the only birds seen.

May 12th.—No dredge was taken. The trap was raised in the afternoon and contained 48 fish of total weight 66½ lbs. The smallest was 9 ozs., and the three largest 3 lbs. 4 ozs., 2 lbs. 14 ozs., and 2 lbs. 6 ozs., and measured respectively 17½ ins., 16½ ins., and 16 ins. Of the remaining 45, the males numbered 15, the females 29, and one, which seemed to be at least a distinct variety, was not determined. On the whole it was impossible to distinguish any definite external characters peculiar to either sex. The only birds seen were paddies and some snowy petrels.

The fo'c'sle paddy now lives quite contentedly in the fo'c'sle all day, often perched on a projecting board under the skylight.

May 13th.—Two hauls of the dredge was taken and contained only two small pycnogons, a large nemertean, a star-fish, a sea-urchin and a tunicate. Paddies and snowy petrels were the only birds observed, although a party of men went round Russ Point where Cape pigeons, nellies and gulls were seen last week.

May 14*th.*—No dredge or trap. Paddies and snowies abundant, the latter numerous on the north beach. Davidson reported a penguin on the ice in Jessie Bay. The paddy is now aboard daily, and usually spends all day long in the fo'c'sle or in the galley.

May 15*th.*—Two hauls of the dredge were taken and contained pycnogons, asteroids, a large holothurian, a large isopod, a large nemertean and sponges. The trap had caught six fish, weighing in all 7 lbs. 9 ozs., three males and three females. The largest was a female weighing 2 lbs. 4 ozs., and measuring 16 ins. in length. Paddies were as usual abundant round the ship and beach, and snowy petrels particularly numerous at the cliffs round at the open water in Uruguay Cove and other parts of Jessie Bay; thirteen were shot. A nelly and a black-backed gull were also seen. The two Weddell seals which were seen last Friday in Jessie Bay were in the same place to-day over against Pirie Peninsula. Another seal blow-hole was also seen.

May 16*th.*—The dredge was very unproductive; only small pycnogons and a large nemertean. The trap contained one fish, a male weighing 1 lb. 6 ozs. The old bait was taken out and fresh penguins bodies put in. From the old bait was obtained a rock-jar full of amphipods. The birds seen were paddies and snowy petrels, the latter in great numbers on different cliffs of Mackenzie, Mossman, and Pirie Peninsulas; no penguins.

May 17*th.*—Paddies and snowy petrels were seen.

May 18*th.*—Twenty fish were caught in the trap. Total weight 23¾ lbs., weight of largest 2 lbs. 5 ozs., length 15¾ ins., female; smallest 5 ozs., length 9¼ ins., sex undetermined; 12 males, 5 females. Those of undetermined sex were preserved. One star-fish in the trap.

The dredge was one of the best for some time, numerous molluscs being caught amongst the weed including one new form resembling *Pecten* and another like a *Lima* in a nest of weed; also a complete dead shell of a form very like *Mya*. Small crustaceans were very numerous and nearly a dozen of the smaller species of isopods; abundant small pycnogons, some with ova attached; three holothurians, all different species; two species of star-fish (one of each); one sea-urchin and one ophiuroid; a few polychaetes and large nemerteans and some fragments of a yellow sponge. Paddies fairly abundant around the ship, and snowy petrels seen flying about the cliffs of Mossman Peninsula.

May 19*th.*—In the trap were eight fish; largest, female, weight 2 lbs. 8 ozs., length 16 ins.; smallest, weight 8 ozs., 10 ins. long. Total about 5 lbs. 5 ozs., two males, three females, three undetermined, the latter preserved. Small catch in dredge and nothing new or of great interest. Several gulls were seen flying around the ship and over Jessie Bay; a black-throated penguin was caught near the ship; it had come south from the open water to the north. A nelly was also seen in Jessie Bay; paddies and snowies as before. Mr Bruce saw a shag flying northward. A male

Zoological Log of Scottish National Antarctic Expedition.

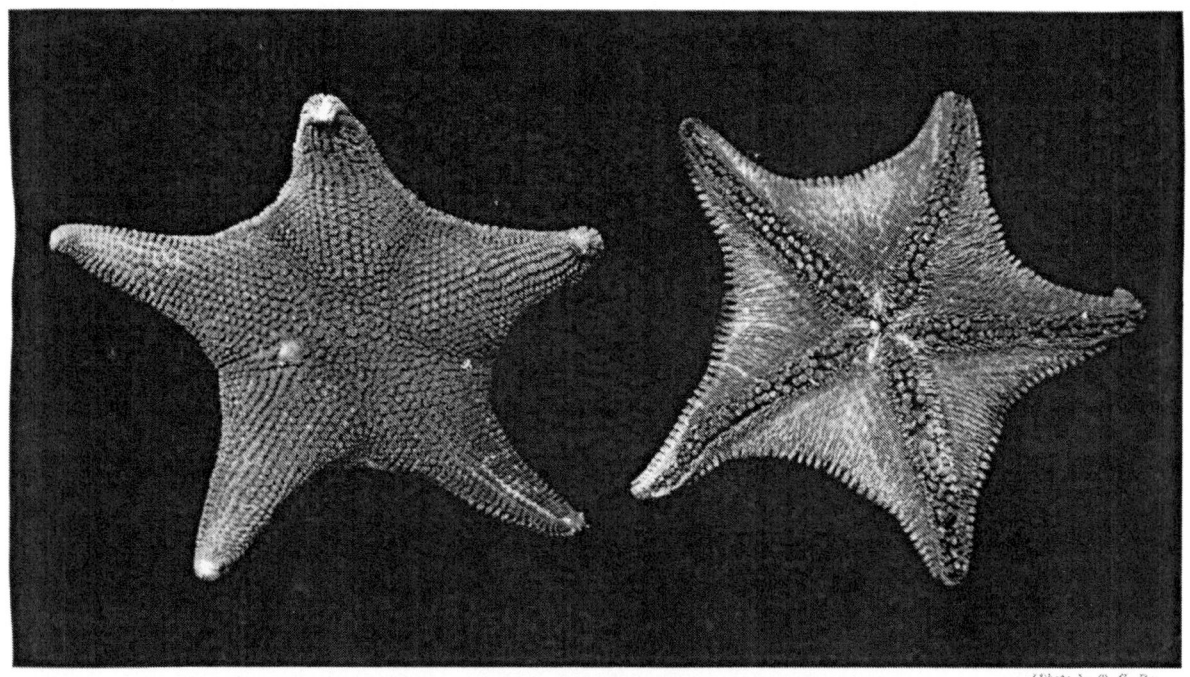

35. The Crimson Cushion Star (*Odontaster validus*).
A shallow water form, of which immense quantities were taken in Scotia Bay in 10 to 30 fathoms.   (1¼ natural size.)

36. A Shallow Water Starfish (*Diplasterias turqueti*), of which considerable numbers were taken in Scotia Bay in 10 fathoms.   (¾ natural size.)

Weddell seal was killed in Jessie Bay and skinned. In its stomach were numerous cepalopod beaks and also nematode worms.

May 20th.—In the trap were thirteen fish, gross weight 13 lbs. 10 ozs.; seven males and six females; largest, a female, 1 lb. 15½ ozs., 15 ins. long; smallest, a male, 5 ozs., length 10½ ins. One of the larger species of isopods was also got. In dredge were one spiny tunicate, one large pycnogon of a dark red colour, and black towards the tips of legs, one large isopod, two holothurians, a star-fish of the salmon-colour species with a lamellibranch within its grasp, apparently being devoured, also small crustaceans, molluscs and eggs, apparently of some mollusc, attached to a piece of sea-weed.

Paddies, and snowy petrels, and some gulls were seen to-day.

May 22nd.—No dredging. The trap to-day yielded 31 fish and three isopods. The heaviest fish weighed 3 lbs. 2 ozs., length 16½ ins., the smallest, a male, weighed 9 ozs., length 10½ ins. The sexes of the fish were eighteen males, eleven females and two undetermined, which latter were preserved. Paddies, snowy petrels and a nelly were seen.

May 23rd.—No dredging. Paddies, snowy petrels, a nelly and some gulls were seen.

May 25th.—The dredge to-day yielded a fair catch; a chiton, lamellibranchs, a gasteropod, several pycnogons, one polychaete and two worm tubes, several star-fishes and cushion-stars, some sertularians and bryozoa and shells on sea-weed. The catch in the trap included thirty-nine fish, one cushion-star and a buckie. The last named animal has not been seen for some time. The fish weighed altogether 48 lbs. 10 ozs. The largest, a female, weighed 2 lbs. 6 ozs., length 16¼ ins.; Mr Bruce made a skeleton of it, as well as of the heads of the next three largest. The next largest was a female, weight 2 lbs. 4 ozs., length 15¾ ins.; the third, a female, weighed 2 lbs. 4 ozs., length 16¼ ins.; the fourth, a female, weight the same, length 15½ ins. (the ova of these last two were in a ripe condition and were bottled); the fifth, a male, weighed 2 lbs. 4 ozs., length 15½ ins. (the milt of this specimen was also bottled as it was in a very ripe condition); the smallest one, a male, weighed 8 ozs., and measured 10¼ ins. in length. Altogether there were 27 females and 12 males. These fish have generally distinct yellow spots on them (like soles) and often present various colours. Paddies, snowy petrels and a nelly have been seen both yesterday and to-day.

May 26th.—A very poor catch, both in trap and in dredge. The dredge contained a few pycnogons, one limpet and some weed with sertularians, bryozoa and a few shells on it. In the trap was a solitary isopod. Snowy petrels and paddies were seen.

May 27th.—Better haul in the dredge to-day, including a nudibranch, three isopods, some pycnogons, two species of star-fish, a holothurian, two species of sponges and sea-weed, with the usual bryozoa, sertularians and shells on it. The trap contained one small fish, a female, and one cushion-star. Put a nelly into the trap for bait, and hope for a better catch next time. Snowy petrels and sheathbills seen.

May 28th.—The dredge contained pycnogons, a polychaete, two star-fishes, some

D

sea-weed and stones with bryozoa, sertularians, and limpets on them.   One stone had a worm tube on it. Nothing in the trap. Copepods were got in a tow-net, through which water was pumped at the dredge-hole. Snowy petrels and sheathbills seen.

May 29th.—Nothing fresh in the dredge except a fish of *Notothenia* type ; the other animals the same as yesterday. We pumped water through a tow-net to obtain a plankton sample, and caught some copepods. Paddies, snowy petrels and gulls were seen.   Mr Bruce saw an immense flock of birds flying over Jessie Bay, which were evidently shags from their colour and size. A Weddell seal was secured near Ailsa Craig for skeleton purposes.

May 30th.—The dredge contained a small octopus, a few pycnogons, three isopods, a polychaete, a sponge, and some sea-weed with the usual epizoa. The trap yielded two fish and a cushion-star. Saw paddies, snowy petrels, shags and gulls.

May 31st.—A large transparent crustacean (*Euphausia*) was seen by Mr Bruce in the dredge-hole. At 3 P.M. an antarctic petrel was seen flying round the ship. Shags, snowy petrels and paddies.

June 1st.—The dredge contained a fish, two or three gasteropods, some pycnogons, including a ten-legged one, a polychaete, three star-fishes, a cushion-star, a holothurian, two sponges, and the usual bryozoa, sertularians and molluscs on sea-weed. Yesterday paddies, snowy petrels and gulls were seen, as well as to-day.

June 2nd.—To-day's dredge was not so rich ; a small fish, a few pycnogons, one sun-star, bryozoa, sertularians, etc. Many black-backed gulls, a nelly, several paddies and snowy petrels were seen. The gulls were particularly noticeable in emitting their typical cry whilst soaring high. In digging through ice on the beach to a depth of four to five feet at the south-east corner of Omond House, part of a shell, a black-throated penguin's skull, a snowy petrel's wing and some weed were found at the bottom of the ice. Limpet shells were also found amongst stones on the talus of Mossman Peninsula.

June 3rd.—The contents of the dredge were richer than yesterday, including limpets, lamellibranchs, two species of isopods, some pycnogons, three star-fishes, two sun-stars and the usual epizoa on sea-weed. A *Euphausia* was also caught in the dredge-hole. Three star-fishes were found on a seal's skeleton which was let down through a hole in the ice on the starboard side of the ship. The trap contained two fish, one of which was a new species, the other of the usual *Notothenia* type, and three sun-stars. Snowy petrels and sheathbills were seen.

June 4th.—The dredge to-day was a fair one ; some pycnogons, two polychaetes, a star-fish, two sun-stars and the usual epizoa on sea-weed and stones. A small trap in the dredge-hole contained two fish and a gasteropod. The trap yielded nine fish. The crew cut a new hole further out in 27 fathoms of water, where the trap was set to-day. Mr Bruce caught three chains of *Doliolum* in this hole, one of which had a small crustacean attached to it, and he also saw some specimens of *Euphausia.*

The weight of the two fish in the small trap was 1 lb. 6 ozs., length 13⅜ ins., and 15 ozs., length 13¼ ins., respectively. The weight of the nine fish was 9 lbs. 5 ozs. The largest one, a female, weighed 1 lb. 12 ozs., and was 15½ ins. in length. Six were females, and three males. Black-backed gulls, snowy petrels, a nelly and paddies were seen.

June 5th.—The catch in the dredge was a poor one to-day. The contents were a small fish, pycnogons, a few star-fishes, one echinoid, some fragments of sponges and a sea-anemone, the last a new species. The usual epizoa on sea-weed. The trap yielded a solitary sun-star. On the surface of the dredge and trap holes numerous examples of *Doliolum* were caught, most of them in chains of from four to twelve, more or less. Found two crustaceans inside two of them, one of which however escaped. Careful drawings and paintings have been made of these animals. Mr Bruce and I saw a Weddell seal near Ailsa Craig. Snowy petrels, paddies and a black-backed gull were seen.

June 6th.—The dredge was not much better than yesterday. It contained a fish, some small pycnogons and a large red one, a worm tube, a large nemertean (not seen for some time past), two sun-stars, fragments of a holothurian and the usual animals on sea-weed. Some examples of *Euphausia* were caught on the surface of the dredge-hole. Whilst killing the anemone caught yesterday, several young came out from under the bell or from the mouth. Snowy petrels, paddies and a nelly were seen.

June 8th.—Very poor haul in the dredge to-day ; one isopod, a few pycnogons, a small star-fish on a stone, and the usual animals on sea-weed. Two fish, a large ctenophore, 5½ ins. × 3 ins. (? *Beroe*), which unfortunately broke up whilst being fixed in 2½ % formalin, and numerous amphipods were in the trap. The small trap in the dredge-hole contained two big sun-stars. Pirie caught plenty of *Euphausia* on the surface of the dredge-hole. The fish caught were both females, of which the larger one weighed 1 lbs. 10 ozs., and measured 15¼ ins. in length ; it was preserved for its ovary. Probably the spawning season is just ended. The other weighed 9 ozs., and measured 10½ ins. Snowy petrels and sheathbills seen both yesterday and to-day. A flight of shags was noticed this morning whilst we were at the trap.

June 9th.—No dredging. Hauled trap up, and got one star-fish and one buckie, then lowered coarse tow-net from surface to 20 fathoms five times. The small trap in the dredge-hole caught some sun-stars and two buckies. No birds seen except one sheathbill. It has been misty and overcast all day.

June 10th.—First haul of the dredge brought up a large sponge. Second haul a few pycnogons, polychaetes and several star-fishes, one of which had encircled a lamellibranch which it was eating, and two or three pieces of sea-weed, amongst which were numerous small crustaceans and fragments of sponges. Again rather misty and no birds seen.

June 11th.—A large holothurian was the conspicuous item of the catch in the dredge to-day, and a painting was made of it. There were also a few pycnogons, some small crustaceans, a polychaete, three star-fishes, an ophiuroid and small lamellibranchs on sea-weed. Nothing in the large trap. *Euphausia* common in the new hole dug to-day for the middle-sized trap. A seal was also seen at the dredge-hole. One nelly, a snowy petrel, two black-backed gulls (one young), two paddies and a shag were seen.

June 12th.—The first haul of the dredge brought up a large red pycnogon, a few ordinary pycnogons, a sea-urchin, an isopod, two stones and a piece of sea-weed ; the next haul was a blank. Only amphipods were in the large trap ; in the middle-sized trap were seven buckies. Lowered coarse net down in hole but got no catch. Obtained specimens of *Euphausia* and *Doliolum* from surface of the trap-hole. Three paddies and a nelly were seen.

June 13th.—One paddy was seen.

June 14th.—No birds were seen.

June 15th.—One small fish, one star-fish and a pycnogon comprised the catch of the dredge. The large trap contained nothing, the middle-sized trap more than a dozen buckies, and the little trap contained some cushion-stars. This trap was shifted from the dredge-hole to a hole cut through the ice in Uruguay Cove, 9 fathoms depth. Three sheathbills were the only birds seen.

June 16th.—The dredge contained two or three small pycnogons, a cushion-star and an ophiuroid—very poor catch indeed. Two paddies were seen.

June 17th.—Rich haul in the dredge consisting of several gasteropods, and many crustaceans in a quantity of weed, pycnogons, isopods, polychaetes, four species of star-fish, large nemerteans, same large holothurian as on the 11th inst., two sea-urchins, four species of star-fish, including a new one which the artist has painted, cushion-stars, two of which are young, and a sponge. The middle-sized trap was hauled up with two buckies and some amphipods in it from 27 fathoms ; these amphipods seem to be more plentiful in water of 27 fathoms than at lesser depths. A tow-net was lowered away in 20 fathoms four times. Eight fish of the usual common species were caught in the small trap set on the 15th in Uruguay Cove, depth 9 fathoms. A parasite was found on the fish. The weight of the eight fish amounted to 6 lbs. 10 ozs., two of them, both females, weighing 1 lb. 1 oz. Five were females (ovary young), three males. Two sheathbills were seen.

June 18th.—Only one sea-urchin, a stone and some weed were got in the dredge. No. 1, the largest trap, contained a fish, which was slightly different from the usual *Notothenia* kind, in having a less square head and a finer mouth ; numerous amphipods both inside and outside the trap. *Euphausia* was seen at the dredge-hole. Amphipods and *Doliolum* were seen at the trap-hole No. 1. No. 3, the small trap in Uruguay Cove, contained three fish, one of which is a new species, the same as caught in trap No. 1 on 3rd inst., and which was carefully painted and preserved ; this one was also preserved. The other three fish, the largest weighing 1 lb. 3 ozs., the next 1 lb. 1 oz., and the new variety 12 ozs., were preserved. Two paddies were seen to-day.

June 19th.—No dredging. A paddy was seen, and Pirie saw some feather balls at the flagstaff on Point Davis, probably indicating gulls.

June 20th.—The contents of the dredge comprised a small fish, which has been

Zoological Log of Scottish National Antarctic Expedition.

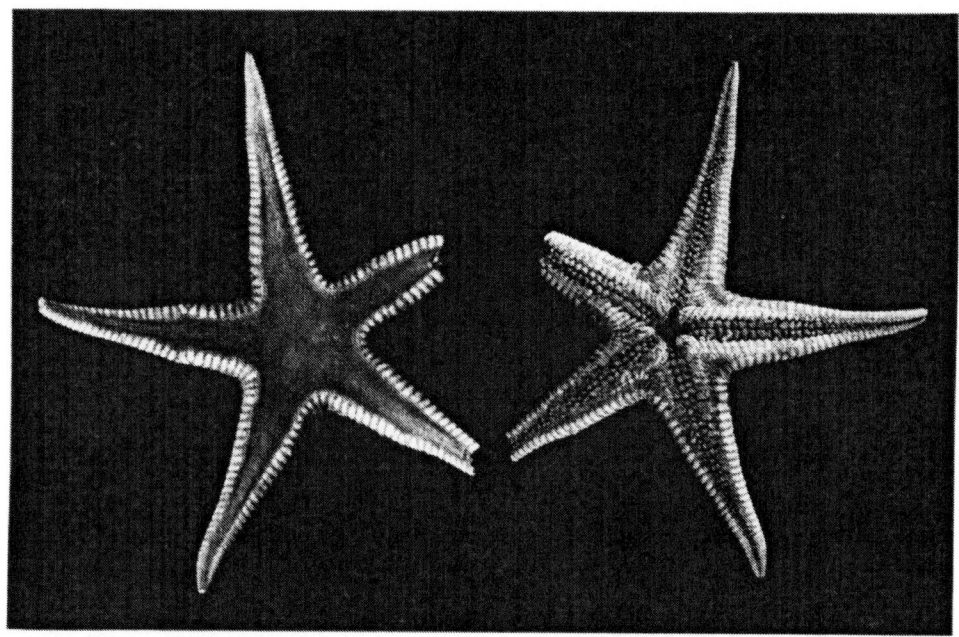

[Photo by T. C. Day.

37. A Deep Water Starfish (*Psilasteropsis facetus*), taken in 1742 fathoms, lat. 48° 6′ S., long. 10° 5′ W.   (⅔ natural size.)

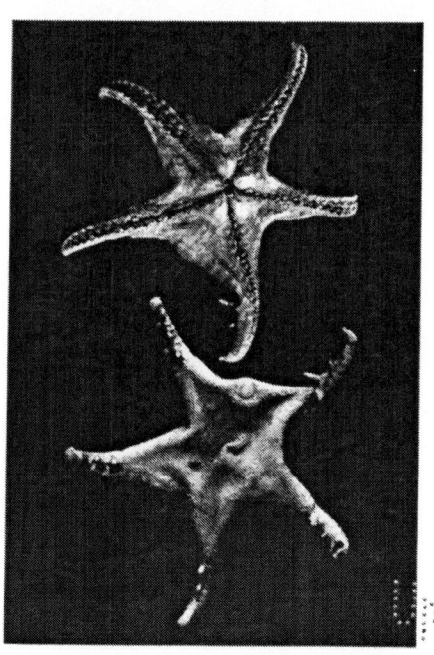

[Photo by T. C. Day.

38. A Deep Water Starfish (*Chitonaster johannæ*),
taken in 1775 fathoms, lat. 62° 10′ S., long. 41° 20′ W.
(⅞ natural size.)

[Photo by T. C. Day.

39. A Deep Water Starfish (*Styracaster robustus*),
taken in 2103 fathoms, lat. 51° 7′ S., long. 9° 31′ W.
(⅞ natural size.)

painted, a limpet, a few pycnogons, a small isopod, three sea-urchins, one of which has been preserved in formalin for its ovary, some star-fish, a holothurian and a small piece of sponge. Traps No. 1 and No. 3 contained nothing. A bird was seen on The Beach, which some thought was a penguin, while others decided it was a nelly; Brown immediately went on shore in pursuit of it, but, whatever it was, it had vanished before Brown's arrival on The Beach. A paddy was seen near the ship.

June 21st.—A penguin (*Pygoscelis adeliae*) was caught this afternoon on The Beach. One paddy was seen.

June 22nd.—Two isopods, a few pycnogons, three species of star-fish and a small gasteropod were obtained in the dredge. No. 3 trap in Uruguay Cove yielded three fishes. The largest, a male, weighed 1 lb. 2 ozs., length 12 ins.; the next, a male, 1 lb., length 11½ ins.; the smallest, a male, weighed 14 ozs., length 11 ins. Eight penguins (all black-throated) were caught near the ship, coming from a southerly direction. Brown and Davidson saw a flock of shags, about forty in number.

June 23rd.—A few pycnogons, a large purple-brown sea-cucumber and a fragment of a sponge were caught in the dredge. Nothing in the trap No. 3; No. 1 trap contained a fish, a buckie and a cushion-star, and the usual large quantity of amphipods, besides another bright red one, probably a new species. Four paddies were seen about the ship, also a snowy petrel flying above Wilton Bay. The fish caught in No. 1 trap measured 12¼ ins. in length, its weight was 1 lb., and it was a male.

June 24th.—Three or four paddies were seen about the ship, and many snowy petrels were seen around Point Martin.

June 25th.—Only a few pycnogons were got in the dredge. Three fish were found in No. 1 trap, weighing altogether 3½ lbs., the largest one weighed 1 lb. 4 ozs., and measured 12¾ ins., the other two were 12 ins., sex undetermined; all three preserved. Two or three paddies about the ship.

June 26th.—Only a few pycnogons in the first haul of the dredge. The second haul was very rich and abundant in species, including a new gasteropod, lamellibranchs, chitons, an isopod, several pycnogons, twelve or more polychaetes, two terebellids with tubes, large nemerteans, a sea-urchin, five star-fish, several brittle-stars, two or three cushion-stars, three holothurians, two pink, and the third a purply-brown one, several sponges, a very great number of minute crustaceans, bryozoa and sertularians on sea-weed. Amongst a clump of weed was a whole nest of large nemerteans. In the trap were four ordinary *Notothenia*, a pair of the new kind (*vide* the 3rd inst.), two isopods, apparently a pair, and an abundance of amphipods, and three worms with suckers were found on the under surface of the larger isopod. This trap was shifted on the 23rd inst. to a new hole further south, in the same depth, 27 fathoms. The ice in Uruguay Cove has been driven out and carried the trap No. 3 with it. A new hole in 10 fathoms has been cut to the south of No. 1 trap-hole but further inshore, and the new trap will be put down to-morrow. The four *Notothenia* weighed 5½ lbs., and were all males, with well developed testes in very ripe condition; they were preserved. They measured 15 ins., 13¾ ins., and 12 ins. respectively. A seal is usually seen at the trap-hole in Scotia Bay, and one was seen by Brown in Uruguay Cove. He angled for it with a *Notothenia*, but it would not bite. No seals but Weddells have been seen since we went into winter quarters. Paddies, snowy petrels, a black-backed gull and a gentoo were seen, the latter swimming in Uruguay Cove.

June 27th.—Only a few pycnogons and some sea-weed in the dredge. Lowered medium-sized trap in hole to the south of No. 1 trap-hole. A few paddies were seen about the ship, and some penguins heard by Pirie in Uruguay Cove. Only two traps are now in use, the new one, No. 2, and the small one, No. 1, No. 3 having been carried away by the ice in Uruguay Cove.

> No. 1 trap.—The large trap, depth of hole 27 fathoms.
> No. 2 trap.—Medium-sized (new), ,,   ,,   10 fathoms.

June 28th.—Hauled up No. 2 trap, which contained thirty-one fish of the ordinary *Notothenia* type, variously coloured, also a considerable number of amphipods. In Buchan Bay, whilst going toward Wilton Bay, Mr Bruce and I saw a bird which was either a young black-backed gull or a skua. In Buchan Bay saw several snowy petrels, and in Wilton Bay saw a seal far off. Russ made him move to his hole. A few paddies were seen about the ship. Total weight of fish, 30 lbs. 2 ozs. (the largest one weighed 2½ lbs.) of which seven were males, twenty females and four undetermined.

June 29th.—Not much in the dredge; a few pycnogons, a chiton, a holothurian and a sea-urchin, and a small quantity of sea-weed. Trap No 1 contained a fish and a buckie; trap No. 2 nineteen fish. Twenty fish weighed 26 lbs. 3 ozs., two of which were males, twelve females and six undetermined. The contents of their stomachs were amphipods, large nemerteans, and some smaller fish of their own kind. In the afternoon trap No. 2 was again lifted and we found ten fish, which weighed 8 lbs. 10 ozs., four being males, five females and one undetermined. Two or three paddies about the ship. A black-backed gull or a skua was seen flying about in the afternoon.

June 30th.—Two or three pycnogons, a star-fish, and some weed were the contents of the dredge. Trap No. 1 yielded a fish and a buckie; No 2, two fish. Numerous amphipods were in both traps. The three fish weighed 1 lb. 14 ozs.; all were preserved. The fish caught on 28th, 29th, and 30th inst. are all the ordinary *Notothenia* common to this place. There is a great variety of colour about them, of which a careful study has been made.

The usual paddies about the ship.

July 1st.—No dredging or trapping. Four paddies about the ship.

July 2nd.—A new fish like the pipe-fish[1] was caught on the surface of the dredge-hole by Davidson; its colour was recorded. A green fish, like the new one caught on

[1] *Notolepis Coatsi* sp. nov.

the 3rd ult., three chitons, three small pycnogons and a large one, an isopod, a polychaete, a young large nemertean, four ophiuroids and a star-fish comprise the catch of the dredge. Trap No. 1 contained amphipods alone. Trap No. 2 contained eight fish, weighing altogether 7 lbs. 6 ozs., three cushion-stars, besides star-fish, a buckie and the usual quantity of amphipods. The eight fish caught to-day in trap No. 2 were all preserved. One fish had three dorsal fins, one had five, and the rest had four.

Whilst out at traps we saw two or three flocks of birds flying over some open water to the west of Ailsa Craig, evidently shags. Three nellies were seen by Mr Bruce and the mate during the course of the day. The usual two or three paddies about the ship. Three snowy petrels and a paddy were seen at trap-hole No. 1. They evidently go there to pick up the amphipods brought up by the trap.

July 3rd.—The dredge contained two isopods, a few pycnogons, one limpet, two lamellibranchs and two or three gasteropods, one chiton, two or three "worms" and a few crustaceans. Trap No. 1 contained a fish and a few amphipods. Trap No. 2, five fish and three cushion-stars, but no amphipods. All the fish were of the ordinary *Notothenia* type. Three have been preserved. The largest one (female) weighed 15 ozs., and measured 12½ ins.; the smallest one (preserved—sex undetermined), 9 ozs., was 10 ins. in length. One weighed 10 ozs. and was 11½ ins. in length (preserved), three weighed a total of 2 lbs. 4 ozs., and were each 11¾ ins. in length, one of which was preserved. Three females, three undetermined, the others male. Two of the fish had five dorsal rays, the rest four.

A number of snowy petrels about the cliffs, one nelly and a black-backed gull, besides the usual paddies were seen. A seal was seen in Jessie Bay.

July 4th.—The first haul of the dredge brought up a large stone with some (?) laminaria[1] "roots" attached to it and a large isopod. On breaking up these roots we found five or six worms, three or four brittle-stars, rather damaged and a small star-fish. On the stone itself a nudibranch with a small pycnogon on it was discovered. The second haul brought up a few blades of sea-weed with nothing on them.

Davidson saw a shag flying northwards past the ship's bows, and the usual paddies were seen.

July 6th.—The dredge brought up a small fish, a large nudibranch, one pycnogon and a star-fish. No. 1 trap contained a fish. No. 2 five fishes and four star-fishes. All the fish were of the ordinary *Notothenia* type, and weighed altogether 5 lbs. 9 ozs. Two of them, a male and a female, had five dorsal fins, the remaining four (one male, three females) had four dorsal fins. Only two or three paddies were seen.

July 7th.—The dredge contained some pycnogons and a few pieces of sponge; rather a poor catch. Nothing in trap No. 1; No. 2 trap contained 54 fish *(Notothenia),*

[1] *Lessonia simulans,* sp. nov.

one of which was the new kind (see June 3rd). The 54 fish weighed 57 lbs. 1 oz., average weight 1·057 lbs., the heaviest fish weighing 2 lbs. 10 ozs., the lightest 4 ozs. Fifteen were males, twenty-seven females, twelve undetermined. The biggest fish were nearly all females, the males being much smaller. The testes of four of the latter were very ripe, especially in one case; the ova of five of the females were in an advanced stage. The twelve sexually undetermined and the new fish were all preserved. The colour of these fish varies very considerably from green to red, brown, copper-red, yellow, orange and grey being also noticed. Twenty-five of these fish had four first dorsal fin rays, twenty-five had five, two had six and one had three. The new fish (see June 3rd) had eight first dorsal fin rays. The contents of the stomachs of the first were small cuttle-fish, 2 ins. or 3 ins. long, *Euphausia* and a buckie minus the shell. The lengths of these fish varied from 17·1 ins. to 7·7 ins., average 12·5 ins.

A flock of shags—about a hundred or so—were seen flying north, also two nellies. The usual paddies about the ship.

July 8th.—Dredge yielded a few pycnogons, a sea-urchin and a broken soft tunicate. Six fish were caught in No. 1 trap, thirty-three in No. 2, all of the ordinary *Notothenia* type. The average weight was 1 lb. 4½ ozs., average length 13·4 ins. Eighteen were females, nine males and twelve undetermined; the latter were preserved. Twenty-three had four first dorsal fin rays, fourteen had five, one had three and one had six dorsal fin rays. Three of the males were quite ready for fertilizing, while four of the females had their ova in a mature stage.

A nelly and the usual paddies were seen. A seal was killed on the ice opposite Point Davis,—a young female with no embryo. On cutting it open, we found some parasitic worms in its stomach, none however in its gut; its duodenum was also filled with parasites which looked like seeds in outward appearance.

July 9th.—A large holothurian, an isopod and some pycnogons were caught in the dredge. Trap No 1 contained a fish and a buckie while trap No. 2 had eleven fish, besides, of course, the usual amphipods in both traps. The fish were all the usual *Notothenia*. Average weight 1 lb., average length 12·06 ins. Five were female, six male and one undetermined. Six had four first dorsal fin rays, five had five and one had six. Three of the males were ready for fertilizing. Brown took the temperature of one of the fish and found it to be 29°·27. A worm was found on the anal fin rays of one of the fish.

A shag, a black-backed gull, a nelly and three paddies were seen.

July 10th.—Tried a new trawl which MacDougall made; lowered it down dredge-hole; did not catch anything with it. Had the dredge down afterwards and caught some pycnogons, a soft tunicate, and an isopod, a young ophiuroid, a young chaetopod and a small amphipod. A red holothurian was caught on the surface of the hole where the seal was lowered. Two or three paddies.

July 11th.—Nothing much in the dredge; have not yet had a decent haul in the dredge this month. Eighteen fish were caught in No. 1 trap, and thirty-four in

Zoological Log of Scottish National Antarctic Expedition.

[*Photo by W. S. Bruce.*

41. Dredging in Deep Water.

[*Photo by R. W. Wilton.*

43. The Large Trap used by "Scotia's" Naturalists.

[*Photo by W. S. Bruce.*

40. Dredging in Shallow Water at Winter Quarters from "Scotia's" bow.

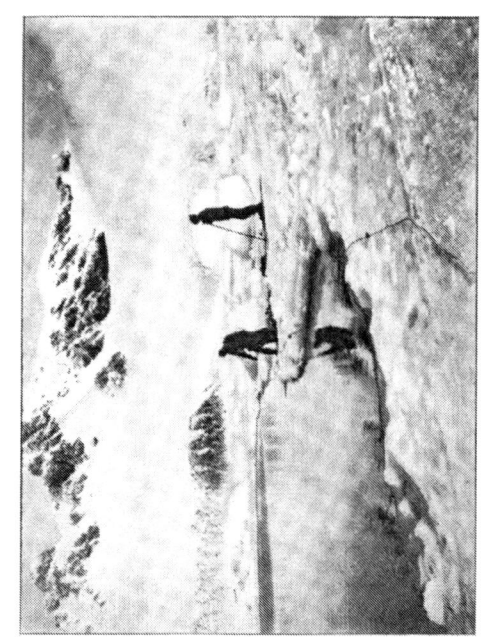

[*Photo by R. N. R. Brown.*

42. Setting a Fishing Line in a Large Pool in Scotia Bay.

No. 2 trap, a total of fifty-two fish. Thirty-three were females, none with ripe ovaries. Twelve male, four of which had their milt in a very ripe condition, and six of undetermined sex. Average weight of the fish was 1 lb. 1 oz. Average length 12·4 ins. Twenty-seven had five first dorsal fin rays, twenty had four and five had three.

Several cushion-stars and star-fish were caught in No. 2 trap. Two amphipods were obtained by means of a small contrivance[1] manufactured by Brown and Gravill, and fastened inside No. 1 trap.

Two or three paddies and a white nelly were seen.

July 12th.—Stabbed a Weddell seal near islet to the south of Point Davis, a very large male with a splendidly marked skin. Saw several other seals lying on the ice, all Weddells. Gulls, a nelly, snowy petrels and paddies seen.

July 13th.—Yesterday's seal was brought to the ship. It is 9½ ft. long.

July 14th.—Brown went out to No. 2 trap, and found thirty-eight fish in it, all *Notothenia*. The average weight was 1 lb. 3 ozs., average length 12·9 ins.—26 females, 12 males. The reproductive organs of the females were not in an advanced stage but several of the males were quite ripe. Twenty-three had four first dorsal fin rays, eleven had five and four had three.

Weather been very windy. Only paddies seen to-day and yesterday.

July 15th.—Took a haul of the dredge this morning; one sponge and a few pycnogons. Paddies seen. Brown saw a snowy petrel. Mr Bruce saw a bird which he thought was a skua, too far off to distinguish clearly.

July 16th.—The first haul of the dredge contained absolutely nothing; the second one was better—best catch in the dredge for this month. It comprised several pycnogons, two isopods, chiton, a limpet, a chaetopod, a large nemertean, a small ophiuroid, two star-fish and several cushion-stars, four holothurians, two sponges, several crustaceans and much weed with animals attached to it. Sixteen fish were caught in No. 1 trap, eighteen in No. 2, besides two cushion-stars; all ordinary *Notothenia*. Average weight 1 lb. 1½ ozs., average length 12·6 ins. Seventeen were female, ten male, seven undetermined. Only one male and one female had their sexual organs in an advanced condition. Twenty had five first dorsal fin rays and fourteen had four. Usual paddies about the ship.

July 17th.—Only two star-fish caught in the dredge. A nelly, a snowy petrel and paddies seen.

July 18th.—A decent catch in the dredge, consisting of limpets, pycnogons, several small crustaceans, a chaetopod, and a large nemertean, several cushion-stars and other star-fish, besides the usual bryozoa and sertularians on sea-weed. Fifty fish were caught in No. 1 trap, and thirty-eight in No. 2, besides two cushion-stars. All fish of the ordinary *Notothenia* type, except two of the green variety. The average weight of the

---

[1] This was a small cylindrical copper framework covered with No. 3 tow-net silk, with a concave funnel opening at either end. The ends were removable to allow the catch to be taken out. Dimensions, 1 foot by 4 or 5 inches.

E

ordinary *Notothenia* was 1 lb. 2¾ ozs., average length 12·2 ins. Twenty-nine were females, thirty-eight males and nine undetermined. Three males and three females had their reproductive organs fairly well developed. Forty-two had four first dorsal fin rays, thirty-one had five, two had six and one had three. Several small fish, red crustacean spawn, large nemerteans, and other beasts were found in these fishes stomachs. A nelly, two black-backed gulls and paddies were seen.

July 19*th*.—Paddies were seen. There is nothing else to record.

July 20*th*.—Only a large star-fish, with young attached, and two or three pycnogons were caught in the dredge. No. 2 trap contained thirteen fish, some cushion-stars and the usual amphipods. The fish were of the ordinary *Notothenia* type. Average weight was 14·9 ozs., average length 11·9 ins. Three male, seven female and three undetermined. Five had five first dorsal fin rays and eight had four. A black-backed gull and paddies were seen.

July 21*st*.—Very poor catch in the dredge ; a few pycnogons, one small isopod, two large nemerteans, and a broken sea-urchin, and some sea-weed with attached bryozoa. One of the large nemerteans ate two pycnogons whilst in a basin in the laboratory. Birds have been seen in greater quantities, possibly because the day has been fine. Some nellies, black and otherwise, black-backed gulls, several snowy petrels and four paddies.

July 22*nd*.—Two large red pycnogons copulating, a sponge with sea-weed growing on it, and some small pycnogons were caught in the dredge. Eighty-seven fish in No. 1 trap, twelve in No. 2, with the usual amphipods in both traps. About a dozen cushion-stars in No. 2 trap. All the fish were of the ordinary type. The average weight of ninety-eight fish was 1½ lbs., average length 13·9 ins. Fifty-six were females, a third of which had their reproductive organs in an advanced stage ; twenty-one were males, a half of which had milt exuding from them ; twenty-one were undetermined. Thirty-six had five first dorsal fin rays, fifty-nine had four, two had three and one had six. The usual various colours were observed in the fish, and their stomachs contained smaller fish, bait (seal) and other matter.

Paddies, snowy petrels, black-backed gulls and nellies were seen during the day, also a skua by Mr Bruce.

July 23*rd*.—Very poor catch in the dredge, only two star-fish, a soft tunicate and three or four pycnogons. Did not go to the traps. Lowered a small trap where soundings are being taken in the middle of Scotia Bay in 37 fathoms. Black-backed gulls, snowy petrels, nellies and paddies were seen. Pirie shot a male Weddell seal and two snowy petrels.

July 24*th*.—Only one cushion-star and five pycnogons in the dredge. No. 1 trap yielded seven fish, No. 2 eleven, and about a dozen cushion-stars. All the fish were of the ordinary type. The average weight of the eighteen fish was 1 lb., average length 12·2 ins. Ten were female, three male and five undetermined (preserved). The sexual organs of neither sex were in a mature condition. Ten had five first dorsal fin rays, six had four, one had six, and one had its first dorsal fin rays bitten, so that one could not tell how many there were. Usual mixed contents of the stomach. Thousands of shags were seen to-day, as well as numerous black-backed gulls, both young and adult, nellies, snowy petrels, and the usual paddies about the ship.

July 25th.—One star-fish and three pycnogons in the dredge. Nellies, black-backed gulls, both young and adult and snowy petrels were seen in great quantities. A gentoo penguin was captured at Point Davis. Weddell seals and a few paddies were also seen. Fitchie killed a male Weddell seal with a pocket-knife ;[1] it had fish and nematode worms in its stomach.

July 26th.—Numerous nellies, one almost pure black, gulls, snowy petrels and five or six paddies were seen.

July 27th.—Brown lifted a small trap which was lowered down in 50 fathoms, muddy bottom ; two fish (*Notothenia*) and numerous amphipods. One of the fish was dead when the trap was hauled up. To-day has been very squally with driving snow ; a few nellies, gulls and sheathbills were seen.

The captive penguin made no objection to sitting for his portrait on the cabin table.

July 28th.[2]—The dredge contained one pycnogon. The traps, between them, twenty-two of the usual fish, several star-fish and many amphipods. A polychaete was also got in the small trap (9¼ fathoms). Several specimens of a species of *Euphausia* were caught on the surface of the trap-hole. Many crimson cushion-stars were taken off a seal's skeleton lowered in about 10 fathoms. Nellies and black-backed gulls seen, as well as snowies and paddies. Many flocks of shags were observed flying towards Saddle Island, several across the bay to the eastward of Brown's Bay, where they appeared to alight in a pool of open water. Three shags flew across Scotia Bay to the southward.

"Charlie "[3] has become quite reconciled to his new home on the monkey poop, where he spends most of his time in quiet meditation or in peaceful slumber. In spite of repeated persuasions, he refuses to accept a drink, and has more than once shown his disapproval of water by overturning a basin of it offered to him. Otherwise he is most sweet-tempered, and calmly allows himself to be subjected to the ordeal of temperature taking.

July 29th.—One pycnogon was the only catch in the dredge. The traps were not examined. Nellies, a black-backed gull, paddies and snowies were seen. A small trap was taken out to the encampment on Delta Island for the investigation of the fauna of that region by Wilton and others. "Charlie " pursues the even tenor of his way, and refuses to allow his dignified composure to be disturbed in any manner.

[1] These seals were always killed by stabbing, as this method was least injurious to the skin.
[2] D. W. Wilton left on a week's sledge trip to Delta Island and Mill Cove. In his absence until August 5th the log was kept by the naturalists remaining on board.
[3] This was the gentoo penguin captured on July 25th.

July 30*th.*—Heavy snow squalls from S.S.W. with driving snow. No dredge or traps. A solitary shag was observed flying westward. No other birds were seen.

July 31*st.*—There was nothing in the dredge. No. 1 trap had nine fish and one star-fish. No. 2 trap had four fish. All the fish were of medium or small size. Total weight of fish 13 lbs. 3 ozs., average length 12·14 ins. One paddy was seen, and a doubtful bird—either a black-backed gull or a nelly. "Charlie" appeared restless and discontented this morning when he was sitting for his portrait. He seemed to be in want of a swim. After lunch he was taken to the dredge-hole and enticed to take a dive, but he persistently refused, and even when he was forced into the water, he scrambled out at once : again and again he declined to stay in the water. Possibly the water appeared too dark to him owing to its being surrounded by thick ice. Perhaps he simply did not feel in the mood for a swim. Now he is peacefully re-established on the monkey poop.

Aug. 1*st.*—The dredge contained one star-fish and three pycnogons. A paddy and a shag were seen, the latter flying southward. A flock of shags, several thousands in number were seen by Mr Bruce—nellies, snowy petrels and paddies as well. A black-throated penguin was captured alive on the beach on its way north, and brought aboard. It is now tied up on the poop, but seems very much to resent its captivity and continually struggles to free itself. "Charlie" seemed to regard "Pathrick's" excitement with contempt and himself retains his composure as of old, only forgetting himself for a moment when "Pathrick" appeared.

A young white seal was found about a quarter of a mile to the south-west. We drove it over to the ship and shot it. It is probably a young *Lobodon carcinophaga* of last year (September). Its side is marked with several deep gashes only very slightly healed. It was noticeable how much quieter and more agile this seal was in its movements than the Weddell seal. The small trap in 51 fathoms was lifted, but had nothing in it but amphipods, mostly of the smaller or younger kind.

Aug. 2*nd.*—Snowy petrels, paddies and shags seen.

Aug. 3*rd.*—No dredging or trapping done to-day. To-day snowy petrels have been seen and heard in the cliffs; no other birds.

Aug. 4*th.*—The dredge contained one star-fish and a few of the common pycnogons. No. 1 trap contained fifty-one fish and one buckie. No. 2 trap contained twenty-two fish and several cushion-stars. All the fish were of the ordinary *Notothenia* type. Average weight was 1 lb. 2·2 ozs., average length 12·8 ins. There were 29 males, 29 females and 15 undetermined. Three of the males were very ripe. Thirty-nine had five first dorsal fin rays, thirty-one had four and two had six, while one was deformed. No. 2 trap was lifted and contained not only numerous cushion-stars, but also hundreds of amphipods. The birds reported to-day are two nellies, numerous snowy petrels and one black-backed gull. No sheathbills were seen. An adelia penguin was caught this forenoon near the ship.

Zoological Log of Scottish National Antarctic Expedition.

[*Photo by W. S. Bruce.*]

45. Animal Life in Deep Antarctic Seas, 1410 fathoms. Weddell Sea 71° 22′ S., 16° 34′ W.

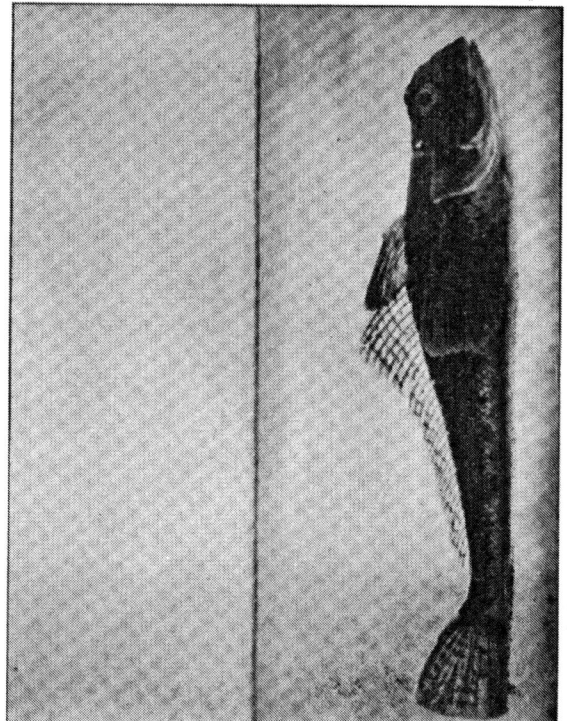

[*Photo by W. S. Bruce*]

47. A Living *Notothenia gibberifrons*, about 10 fathoms, Jessie Bay, South Orkneys. (⅓ natural size.)

[*Photo by W. S. Bruce.*]

44. Animal Life in Shallow Antarctic Seas, 10 fathoms, Scotia Bay, South Orkneys.

[*Photo by T. C. Levy.*]

46. The *Notothenia corriceps*, taken in great numbers in Scotia Bay, 15 to 80 fathoms, also off Coats Land 160 fathoms. (⅓ natural size.)

Aug. 5th.—One spotted star-fish and two or three pycnogons were the only contents of the dredge. No birds were reported; very windy and mild weather.

Aug. 6th.—The dredge yielded the richest catch we have had for some considerable time—gasteropods, pycnogons, polychaetes, several large nemerteans, seven or eight star-fish, a holothurian, three sponges, besides a quantity of sea-weed with attached bryozoa and sertularians on it, and also containing some amphipods and large nemerteans.

A black-backed gull and snowy petrels are the only birds reported to have been seen, probably owing to the wet and misty weather. Mossman and Smith saw a young Weddell seal in Jessie Bay.

Aug. 7th.—A cephalopod, with two parasites attached, a few pycnogons, a cushion-star, with young adhering to it, and another star-fish comprised the contents of the dredge.

Snowy petrels and a paddy have been seen.

Aug. 8th.—Only one large nemertean and three pycnogons were caught in the dredge. Several black-throated penguins were seen going to Jessie Bay. The temperature of two of these birds was taken, and in each case it was 106°. Several snowy petrels, one shag and a black-backed gull were also seen. Snowy petrels were also heard amongst the cliffs at 9 P.M. No paddies.

Aug. 9th.—Four penguins (adelia) were caught to-day, whilst two escaped from the clutches of the leader and the botanist.

Aug. 10th.—Two star-fish and six pycnogons were caught in the dredge. Thirteen fish and amphipods were the contents of No. 1 trap, which was shifted to another hole, depth 54 fathoms. All the fish were of the ordinary *Notothenia* kind. Average weight 14½ ozs., average length 12 ins. Seven were females, five males and two of them of undetermined sex. One of the males had its reproductive organs in a very advanced condition. Eight had five first dorsal fin rays, five had four and one had six. Many amphipods were brought from the traps and preserved. Two penguins were caught to-day. Snowy petrels and one paddy were seen. Stabbed a young male Weddell seal off Point Davis; skin very prettily marked.

Aug. 11th.—Several pycnogons, one pale yellow star-fish, two bright red crustaceans, much weed with a considerable number of animals attached to it, bryozoa, etc., were the contents of the dredge. A worm, probably a large nemertean, was found on the seal's skeleton, rather damaged. One paddy, several snowy petrels, two nellies and two black-backed gulls were the birds seen to-day.

Aug. 12th.—No dredging or trapping to-day; every sailor busy landing stores. About six black-backed gulls, one flock of shags, two or three nellies and several snowy petrels were seen.

Aug. 13th.—The dredge contained three pycnogons and one cushion-star; a small trap in 13 fathoms near the ship, which has been down a week, was lifted to-day and contained two buckies, one yellow star-fish, a large brown star-fish (the largest of its kind we have got yet), six isopods, and 229 crimson cushion-stars, as well as six fish (totalling 5 lbs. 3 ozs.), of which the largest, a female, was 2 lbs. 9 ozs., 17 ins. long. Several black-backed gulls, two nellies, myriads of snowies and a paddy comprise the birds seen to-day.

NOTE.—The small trap brought back last week from the camp at Delta Island caught, while out there, sixteen fish (total 10 lbs.), six cushion-stars and an isopod. Probably more cushion-stars were caught but not brought in.

Aug. 14th.—The only contents of the dredge were a few pycnogons and a star-fish. No birds except a snowy petrel appear to have been seen.

Aug. 15th.—A strong gale. The dredge contained several pycnogons, a limpet, a lamellibranch (formerly only recorded from a broken shell), and a fish which is a new variety probably, if not a new species. The two latter are being painted. The trap in 13 fathoms contained 120 cushion-stars, five isopods, six buckies and seven fish (4 lbs. 8 ozs.). The cushion-stars have a very rugged appearance on their upper surface, which may be due to their having been allowed to expand fully their paxillae in water. No. 1 trap in 54 fathoms contained a small isopod, a new amphipod and six fish.

Aug 16th.—Snowy petrels and black-backed gulls have been seen to-day.

Aug. 17th.—The dredge contained pycnogons, an isopod, small black lamellibranchs and bryozoa on weed. The small trap in 13 fathoms contained ninety-nine cushion-stars, of which seven were kept, including one with four limbs, and one with a bifurcated limb, three isopods, three fish (total 2 lbs.) and two buckies. From the large trap in 54 fathoms were got three fish (total 3 lbs. 3 ozs.) and many amphipods, including one specimen of the new species of August 15th. This trap was brought to the ship as the break-up of the ice at the mouth of the bay rendered its safety doubtful. The birds seen were several nellies, many snowies and black-backed gulls, and possibly an antarctic petrel. Almost all the birds, including the last, were seen at the open water.

At the big trap-hole a large male Weddell seal was found, but it was suffered to depart in safety.

Aug. 18th.—A new fish, which the artist has painted, some entomostracans, two species of isopods, bryozoa, some small lamellibranchs and a star-fish were the contents of the dredge. Some snowy petrels and a flock of shags were seen. Weather has been misty all day.

Aug. 19th.—No trap or dredging to-day. Only one black-backed gull was seen. Still misty and overcast.

Aug. 20th.—Many pycnogons and one star-fish were the contents of the dredge. Davidson caught a holothurian in the dredge-hole. Numerous shags and two black-backed gulls were seen during the day. Mossman saw fifteen gentoo penguins land on The Beach this afternoon from Jessie Bay.

Aug. 21st.—A few pycnogons, one star-fish and a limpet were in the dredge. Six gentoos from Jessie Bay, and many black-throated penguins were seen during the day on the floe and beach, besides a great quantity of shags, which were flying about the cliffs, sitting on the rocks and on the water, as if intent on staying, several snowy petrels and many black-backed gulls. Pirie saw many seals whilst sounding along the edge of the old ice, three of which were sea-leopards, most were Weddells, and possibly some were *Lobodons*. The sea-leopards had made some holes in the bay ice, and were constantly coming up to breathe, sometimes putting out the whole of their head to have a look round, at other times just shoving their nostrils level with the surface of the water. A sea-leopard was observed to catch a black-throated penguin by the leg and haul him down in the water. Several photographs were taken of the seals in their blow-holes.

Aug. 22nd.—One pycnogon and an isopod were found in the dredge. The trap which is lowered in a hole near the ship in 13 fathoms contained two fish, *Notothenia*. One weighed 2 lbs. 7 ozs., and was 17·2 ins. in length, a female. The other, which was preserved, weighed 10 ozs., and had a length of 10·6 ins. Also two yellow star-fish, 174 cushion-stars, one with six arms, and one with four arms, and four buckies.

A Weddell seal thrust its head and shoulders through the trap-hole to have a look round. A flock of shags flying in Jessie Bay, one black-throated penguin, several snowy petrels and four black-backed gulls were reported as having been seen during the day.

Aug. 24th.—One red pycnogon with ova attached, a few small pycnogons, one large nemertean and one small star-fish in the dredge. The trap contained five fish (*Notothenia*) weighing 3½ lbs., three isopods, one gasteropod, one large yellow or orange star-fish and about 100 cushion-stars. The three seals skeletons in a hole by the ship were hauled up; very few amphipods were found on them; in fact, a great scarcity of these beasts prevails near the ship; two large nemerteans and an isopod were also on the carcases. One nelly, a black-throated penguin, several snowy petrels and black-backed gulls were seen during the day. Two of the snowy petrels were observed taking a bath among the slush, one by Pirie, the other by Mossman. Five *Lobodons* and a Weddell were seen in a group by Pirie during sounding operations. Pirie shot a young male *Lobodon*. The *Lobodons* travel faster over the snow than the Weddells. A Weddell seal put up its head in the trap-hole; they are evidently on the eve of returning to land for pupping.

Only snowy petrels and black-backed gulls were seen yesterday.

Aug. 25th.—The dredge contained a small nudibranch, several pycnogons, two yellow star-fish (orange colour in the middle), one sea-urchin and some sea-weed, containing several species of gasteropods, lamellibranchs, and entomostracans,—amongst the root of the weed was a small chiton, a polychaete, several large nemerteans, and two other " worms " (species unknown) were found. We hauled up the trap to get some skeletons[1], and found several cushion-stars. One snowy petrel and one black-backed gull were seen.

Aug. 26th.—Only one star-fish was in the dredge. The Giesbrecht net was lowered away this afternoon to a depth of 6 feet from the surface with very poor results. Pirie saw many *Lobodons* and Weddells during sounding operations. Snowy petrels and black-backed gulls have been seen during the day.

[1] The traps were baited with penguin and other carcases.

Aug. 27th.—One nudibranch and two pycnogons in the dredge. Some black-backed gulls, some snowy petrels and also a nelly have been seen during the day. A hole was made in the bay ice about three-eighths of a mile from the ship towards Point Davis, and three seals skeletons were lowered down. These skeletons have been in a hole near the ship for a fortnight, but have hardly been touched, owing to the absence or scarcity of amphipods in the vicinity of the "Scotia." The trap contained 164 cushion-stars, weighing 6 lbs. 11 ozs. (one star had four arms), three isopods, two buckies, one large nemertean, one yellow star-fish and six fish, all of the *Notothenia* kind, weighing 4 lbs. 10 ozs. Average length 11·4 inches, average weight 12.3 ozs. Brown saw a seal, though too far off to distinguish the species. Five cushion-stars and an isopod were obtained from the seals skeletons.

Aug. 28th.—One small fish and four pycnogons were the contents of the dredge. A nelly and some snowy petrels were seen, also a seal by Pirie, but it was too far off to distinguish the species. Hauled Giesbrecht net up, contents nil.

Aug. 29th.—The first haul of the dredge was a very rich one, the second blank. The first haul contained a small fish, several lamellibranchs and gasteropods, three isopods and several smaller crustaceans amongst sea-weed, two polychaetes and another "worm," several cushion-stars and three or four orange star-fishes, also two small holothurians, several fragments of sponges, including two species, as well as five or six tunicates, a few pycnogons, one with ova attached and much sea-weed with bryozoa, sertularians, etc., on it. Mossman saw a shag flying northwards; a nelly and some snowy petrels were also seen.

Aug. 30th.—The first young seals were seen to-day. At Point Martin three Weddell seals and their young ones were found. Each seal had one pup, probably born to-day or yesterday. The smallest was from 2½ to 3½ feet long. Their coats are woolly and grey-white; as yet they are free from the usual spots and marks on the coats of the Weddell seals. The young have the usual disproportionate head, and their flippers, the hind ones particularly, are well developed, and out of proportion to the rest of the body. The eyes have the characteristic look, large, brown and slightly blood-shot in the white. They move exactly like the adults, but a few yards at a time tires them, and they have to rest. The mother lies alternately on one or the other side when suckling the pup, and, at other times, seems to shelter it by lying to windward. The mother is more fierce, and resents any annoyance more than in her childless state, but one, on being worried with sticks, tried to burrow into the snow as if in search of water, which would have entailed her abandoning her pup. The pup frequently gives a cry, not unlike the bleating of a lamb, but with at times a more human sound about it. The mother too gives vent often to the peculiar hoarse roar, though often the noise more resembles a loud cackle.

All three seals and their young were lying about the line of tide-cracks so that in event of floe giving way a retreat to the land would be quite easy.

A nelly, snowy petrels and black-backed gulls were seen.

Aug. 31st.—The first haul of the dredge contained a few sea-weeds with no animals ; in the second haul there were two pycnogons, a polychaete and a star-fish. Only one nelly seen to-day, by the captain. The rest of us did not see any birds although I was out in the morning and a party were out later securing two young Weddell seals.

According to one of the men who was out with the party securing the two baby seals, the youngest one's mother followed the sledge containing her progeny as far as she was able, emitting no noise or cry, whilst the older one's mother was got rid of much more easily. She escaped through a blow-hole and abandoned her young after a short struggle. The youngest baby seal was killed by chloroform and preserved for its skin ; and the other one was injected and embalmed according to Professor David Hepburn's method,[1] which Pirie and Brown successfully carried out.

Sept. 1st.—The first haul of the dredge contained nil, the second one a cushion-star and a pycnogon. Mr Bruce saw a nelly this morning, the only bird seen to-day. Birds have been very scarce these last two days, probably owing to the cold weather we have been experiencing. Mr Bruce, Cuthbertson and myself were out this afternoon at Point Davis, near where, on the floe, we saw a Weddell seal with her young. On our near approach the mother became alarmed and tried to drive us off ; she was exceedingly fat and moved slowly. Seeing that her efforts were of no effect, she returned to her young and began to caress it by putting her nose to the young one's side, opening her mouth and barking. Satisfied that the young one was all right, she lay down on her side whilst the youngster moved towards her head, where it lay embracing the mother with a flipper. After a while the youngster shifted its position and moved towards the hind end of its parent. Some photographs were taken of mother and young by Mr Bruce.

Sept. 2nd.—The dredge contained not even a pycnogon in either of the two hauls. Only one bird seen—a snowy petrel, by the captain.

The Weddell seal with its young, which we saw yesterday off Point Davis, was brought to the ship. Both were preserved for skins.

Sept. 3rd.—Both hauls of the dredge came up empty. No birds seen. The cold spell we have been experiencing is probably the cause. Yesterday the mean temperature was – 22° F. To-day the temperature has varied more than yesterday, in the afternoon rising to 8°, but at 7 P.M. it was – 20°, with a strong breeze blowing since noon.

Sept. 4th.—No dredge to-day, nor were any birds seen. Cold spell still continuing.

Sept. 5th.—The dredge contained one yellow star-fish with a lamellibranch attached to it. The Giesbrecht net was hauled up empty. The trap was hauled up also and contained four or five fish *(Notothenia)*, kept for skeletons, about 100 star-fish, all cushion-stars, four or five isopods and a few buckies. A nelly and a snowy petrel were seen to-day. The weather has become quite moderate again.

[1] In accordance with a formula presented to the Expedition by Professor David Hepburn, M.D., University of Wales.

F

Sept. 6th.—A nelly was seen by Mr Bruce, and Mossman heard a snowy petrel. Weather quite mild.

Sept. 7th.—A star-fish and several pycnogons were caught in the dredge, also a piece of sea-weed with attached bryozoa.

Brown and I went out to Point Martin to secure a young Weddell seal. We saw four Weddell seals, two with young ones and two about to give birth. We had no difficulty in securing a young one from its mother who did not follow us. On approaching the second seal with a young one to take some snap-shots, we had to keep an eye on her as she several times tried to attack us on our nearer approach. The young was killed by prussic acid. Its temperature was taken a little while after the dose was given : first reading was 97°·6 ; about five minutes afterwards the temperature was taken twice, both times registering 99°·2, which is doubtless the correct reading.

Pirie examined the young seal's eye through an ophthalmoscope and found the colour to be slatey. Two snowy petrels were seen.

Sept. 8th.—No catch in the dredge. Weather still cold, though very clear. Went out again to Point Martin and saw the four Weddell seals we saw yesterday ; no further developments had taken place. We crossed over the spit and saw several other Weddell seals, all with young. Two of them tried to drive us away ; the third mother stayed by its young, and on our second approach gave it several bites about the head and neck, and finally took a good grab of it by the mouth and shook its baby like a dog worries a rat. We interposed on the young one's part and took it from its mother and home to the ship. The poor baby was very much damaged, so we killed it almost immediately. The skin was much whiter than any we had yet seen, but owing to the scars caused by the bites of its mother, it was decided to keep the specimen for skeletal purposes.

Some of the big females are much darker and with more pronounced spots than the others. When disturbed they bark, and sometimes emit a sort of gurgling sound which is generally accompanied by foaming at the mouth. No males have been seen since the females have started pupping. All the females that we have seen with young or about to become mothers have been always on ice close to land. The little bay north of Point Martin seems a favourite place for them when with young.

Three black-backed gulls, two nellies and two snowy petrels were seen to-day.

Sept. 9th.—Two orange star-fish and one cushion-star were in the dredge. The Giesbrecht net was hauled up ; contents nil. Lifted the three seals' skeletons from a hole where they had been for more than fifteen days, and lowered them down in the hole cut for the Giesbrecht net. There were two fishes *(Notothenia)* and a large number of amphipods on the carcases, though they had not made much impression on them. A snowy petrel, a nelly and a shag were reported as having been seen.

Sept. 10th.—A few pycnogons and a star-fish were in the dredge. Went out in the afternoon to look at two seals' skeletons which were lowered down in a hole near " Sounding rock." Caught a big fish *(Notothenia)*, weight 1 lb., and a very small one

Zoological Log of Scottish National Antarctic Expedition.

[Photo by W. S. Bruce.

48. Weddell Seal (*Leptonychotes weddelli*) and Newly-born Young,
Scotia Bay, South Orkneys.

[Photo by W. S. Bruce.

49. Weddell Seal and Young, about two or three days old,
Scotia Bay, South Orkneys.

[Photo by W. S. Bruce.

50. Young Weddell Seal, one day old.

[Photo by T. C. Day.

51. Young Weddell Seal, two days old.

which looked like a miniature *Nototthenia*; several cushion-stars and many amphipods were also on the carcases.

Went out to Point Davis and had a look at the Weddell seals with their young. Brought home a young one. The two mothers whom we had previously deprived of their young were still at the same place—had not taken to the water yet. The first one's young was taken on Monday, the 7th inst., and the other one's on the 8th inst. Three or four snowy petrels, two nellies and three black-backed gulls were seen.

Sept. 11th.—Some *Serpula* on weed and a sea-urchin with well developed testes were in the dredge. Two flocks of shags, several black-backed gulls, nellies and snowy petrels were seen during the day. The dredge-hole has been blasted for some distance, so that we will not be able to do any more dredging for the present.[1]

Sept. 12th.—The baby seal, which we brought to the ship on the 10th inst., is still thriving, though it has not taken nourishment freely; a little milk was forced down its throat.

Snowy petrels, nellies, black-backed gulls and shags were seen, and some gentoo penguins landed from Jessie Bay.

Sept. 13th.—The same birds seen as yesterday. The seal is getting more sociable and likes to be petted. Pirie rigged up a feeding bottle, which, however, baby seal does not understand.

Sept. 14th.—The baby seal has at last taken to the bottle. She (the baby is a female) took about a pint of milk, and does not cry so much. Her crying is sometimes very like a human baby's. More gentoo penguins arrived on The Beach from the north. Snowy petrels, black-backed gulls and two shags were seen.

Sept. 15th.—I was too premature in writing yesterday that the seal took to the bottle; she sucked at it for a very little time, and to-day refused the bottle altogether, so milk was poured down her throat.

Pirie, from a boat in Uruguay Cove, shot three shags and a black-backed gull. The shags were in splendid condition and had a far better plumage than in the autumn. The cere was very prominent, colour cadmion; round the eye there was a patch of cobalt colour. A tuft of feathers ornamented the crest of the bird; the colour of its feet and legs were light scarlet. The artist made a very good painting of its head. The black-backed gull had, besides the yellow of its lower jaw, a patch of crimson on either side; the gape was also tinged with crimson. Numerous snowy petrels, black-backed gulls, one in its young or mottled plumage, shags, four nellies and two gentoo penguins were seen. In the afternoon I shot two shags. A Weddell seal was also seen in Uruguay Cove close in-shore. Limpets and yellow star-fish were seen on the sea-bottom and one pycnogon frozen in the pan-cake ice.

Sept. 16th.—Hauled up the trap from the hole on the port bow, depth 11 fathoms. In it were four fish *(Nototthenia)*, 125 cushion-stars and an isopod. Also hauled up the

---

[1] At this time we were attempting to blast and cut a canal through the floe to the open water beyond, hoping to liberate the ship.

seals' skeletons from the hole where the Giesbrecht net was lowered, depth 14 fathoms. Several amphipods were on the carcases. Snowy petrels and four black-backed gulls were seen.

Baby seal's umbilical cord came off to-day.

Sept. 17th.—Only one nelly and a gentoo penguin were seen. Mossman saw two penguins on the ice in Jessie Bay. The baby seal still refuses to take food freely.

Sept. 18th.—Two or three black-backed gulls and a few snowy petrels were seen to-day. The baby seal still refuses food, so we filled a football bladder with milk and by means of a tube poured the milk straight into its stomach.

Sept. 19th.—Nellies, snowy petrels, black-backed gulls, two penguins (too far off to distinguish species) and two shags were seen during the forenoon. In the afternoon the weather became misty. We feed the seal by means of the football bladder three times a day ; each meal consists of ¾-pint unsweetened milk.

Sept. 20th.—Nellies, snowy petrels and black-backed gulls were seen many times during the day. The baby seal was seized with convulsions before breakfast this morning, and by 8 P.M. she was dead. Brown, Mossman and I· went out this afternoon towards the penguin rookery at Point Martin to have a look at the seals with their young. Near the point on which the rookery is situated we saw about a dozen seals, nine with young ones. One had just given birth, and while we were looking at it, the placenta came away, which Brown secured and brought to the ship. None of the mothers tried to kill or injure their young ones on our near approach, though in one or two cases they tried to drive us away. Some of the young ones were evidently two or three weeks old, others about as many days, and one was just born, the colour of which was dark, and the length about 2 feet 6 inches. We saw one youngster much lighter in colour than the others. Three of the seals we saw were without young ; from two of them I believe we had already taken their young, whilst the third seemed about to give birth. All these seals were *Leptonychotes weddelli*, and in this case, as on previous occasions, we did not see any males.

Sept. 21st.—Round about Delta Island saw over two dozen Weddell seals, of which number one was a male, lying about 100 yards distant from the females. The rest were all females, and as far as we could see every one had a young one with it ; some of the youngsters were much older than the others. We also noticed the two different colours of the young ones—some of a lighter colour, others darker. Only one of the mothers tried to damage its young on our approach ; we, however, instantly moved off, fearing for the cub's life, and did not go near the mother who was immediately appeased. The other mothers greeted us with the characteristic Weddell seal's bark and the peculiar noise which they make when anyone goes near them. They also attempted to drive us away, failing which they moved off for a little distance. I noticed one little one lying asleep with its nose and half its head buried in the snow. Several snap-shots were taken of the seals.

We also saw about six more Weddell seals in Mill Cove and at Cape Nan Anderson, one of which was a male. Three paddies amongst the seals round Delta Island, feeding on their excrement, and, probably, placentae ; they approach quite close to the seals and evidently do scavenger work. Mr Bruce and I saw an almost white black-backed gull ; the colour of its wings on the upper surface was much lighter than is usually the case with these gulls. Some nellies and a good many snowy petrels were also observed ; one of the former appeared to be quite white.

A party went off to Point Martin to capture a young seal with its mother. The young, pupped yesterday, was captured, but its mother, though wounded, escaped down an unnoticed seal-hole, despite the determined hold Fitchie had of her tail and hind flippers. One was then killed who appeared to be pregnant, but, on being cut up, no young was found. It must have been one of these previously robbed and who had since changed her position. It was noticed that on both occasions the first impulse of the wounded seal was to make for its nearest neighbour, who at once put herself in front of her young. The two mothers met, reared up and snarled at one another, and then separated without coming to actual blows. In both cases this happened. Snap-shots of seal and young taken. The female brought in was the largest Weddell yet taken. Length 10 feet 4 inches and weight 920 lbs. (under-estimate probably). Its food, from the contents of the stomach, had been cuttle-fish, fish and holothurians. Many nematodes in the gut.

Sept. 22nd.[1]—Messrs Bruce, Wilton, Pirie and Cuthbertson left this morning for Cape Dundas, and will be absent some days. A small trap accompanied the party. Nellies and black-backed gulls were hovering about in the vicinity of the seal carcases.

The trap in 13 fathoms off the port bow was lifted and contained six isopods, five fish, two yellow star-fish and 210 cushion-stars, one of which had four perfect arms and fifth arm weakly developed.

Martin, Ross and I left in the morning for surveying in Buchan Bay. From Point Martin southward along the shores of Scotia Bay mother seals with and without young were very plentiful—about the shore line and hummocks in Buchan Bay they were particularly numerous. A few made for us if we approached but in most cases they only opened their eyes and stared at us without any alarm. No sign of them trying to injure their young was noticed in any case. No young without a parent was seen, which makes it improbable that during nursing the adult takes the water. None of the adults, now or in any case noticed this last month, were scarred. No males seen.

Nellies were plentiful, feasting on the blood and excrement at the scenes of birth. In one case we saw six nellies sitting round a seal where the young had just been born, probably waiting for the placenta. No sign of any attempt of the nellies on baby seals was seen, although I looked carefully for evidence on this point.

Two paddies were also seen in Buchan Bay feeding on excrement. Birds seen were many gulls, nellies, snowies and two paddies.

[1] During the absence of D. W. Wilton with a sledge party, this log was kept by R. N. Rudmose Brown until October 12th.

Sept. 23rd.—A strong easterly and south-easterly blizzard all day. No birds seen.

Sept. 24th.—While surveying around Cape Burn-Murdoch, saw many Weddell seals, of which most had young. No males were seen nor any young without mothers. It was noticeable that the head of the Weddell seal varies somewhat in shape, and though usually blunt in front, in some specimens is more prolonged, and in these cases the head bears some resemblance to that of *Lobodon carcinophaga.* A mother seal was killed to-day and its young captured alive. The brain of the adult has been taken out and preserved. The young seal is much whiter than the majority of the other pups.

Numerous gulls and snowy petrels were seen and two or three nellies.

Sept. 25th.—Northerly wind and snow. Snowy petrels seen to-day.

Sept. 26th.—Heavy snowfall and southerly wind to-day. Snowy petrels seen. The young seal is still alive but refuses to suck, although the cook forces him to take some nourishment by pouring it down his throat.

Sept. 27th.—Gravill and I went out to look at the seals and young this forenoon. The young seem to prefer to lie to leeward of their mothers, though it can hardly be said that even at birth they seem to feel the cold. The young apparently use their fore-flippers far more than the adult, and often we have seen a pup who appeared to be scratching his head with his hand, or else simply playing. From measurement of young and adult it is noticeable that the fore-flippers of the former are almost the size of the latter, while the hind-flippers of the former are much smaller than these of the latter.

Walker saw a seal pupping on Thursday. He says it took about ten minutes, and that the mother roared almost continually during it. The umbilical cord was severed by the young seal breaking it during birth; it was not bitten through by the mother.

Snowies and black-backed gulls seen to-day.

Sept. 28th.—Snowies, black-backed gulls and several nellies were seen to-day. The young seal on board is prospering and getting quite strong and energetic. The cook feeds him regularly at frequent intervals with porridge, though it has to be poured down his throat. He spends much of his time on the floe and frequently travels round the ship.

Sept. 29th.—Birds seen were snowy petrels, black-backed gulls and nellies.

Sept. 30th.—Snowy petrels were seen and also a nelly which several times alighted near the ship, attracted doubtless by the cran of a seal there.

Oct. 1st.—Snowy petrels seen to-day and also a Cape pigeon which settled on the floe near the ship for some time. The baby seal continues to thrive. He lives chiefly on the floe now, and is getting quite used to being handled, which he no longer resents. He now recognises the cook who generally feeds him.

Oct. 2nd.—Snowies and a black-backed gull seen. Young seal apparently in good health.

Oct. 3rd.—Gulls, nellies and two or three paddies seen to-day, the latter in the vicinity of the seals at the mouth of the bay. Saw many seals, practically all with pups, between Capes Martin and Burn-Murdoch. There was only one which possibly had not yet pupped. The pups are beginning to take the water. I saw one go down a seal hole and remain in the water several minutes, but visible all the time, and occasionally putting its nose up to breathe. On coming up it moved towards its mother, who was sleeping a few yards away, and she greeted it affectionately with a rub of her nose. The woolly coat was still on the pup and showed no signs of coming off yet. Many of the pups were to be seen playing with the mother, the pup using mostly its fore-flippers, the mother using chiefly her head, but no attempted destruction of young or any approach to it could be seen in any case. We saw two pups left by their mothers who were probably away fishing. The pups were asleep, but one appeared to be teething, and on waking up began to rub its gums repeatedly on the hard snow.

Two gentoos captured coming from the southward.

Oct. 4th.—Snowy petrels and gulls seen to-day.

Oct. 5th.—Snowy petrels and gulls were the only birds seen to-day. The captain saw a seal on the floe half way to Point Davis near an old trap-hole ; but as it was seen from the mast-head, the sex could hardly be determined ; no young was visible.

The trap in 13 fathoms on the port bow was raised and contained two fish, one buckie, two isopods, 156 cushion-stars and about twelve amphipods, one of which had four arms. A seal skeleton down a week was hauled up this afternoon. On it were eighteen cushion-stars, one of which had an arm undeveloped, and three fishes.

The baby seal, having died, was skinned and the brain removed and preserved, but the latter was very soft and is not in good condition.

Oct. 6th.—Snowies, black-backed gulls and a nelly were seen to-day.

Oct. 7th.—There is open water to the south and the penguins are arriving in the bay. I spent the day round about Point Martin surveying, and found over forty black-throated penguins about there, some in flocks and some singly. Most of them were climbing up the rocks into old rookeries as if they had come to stay. They were all plump and in very fine condition. They travelled quickly from the water to the rookeries, and I saw two different flocks moving on their bellies at full speed. The seals seemed disinclined to meddle with them, and even one thrown at a seal was untouched, although it stood afterwards for several minutes within a few feet and easy reach of the seal. We then put it down a seal hole and drove the seal in after it. The seal did not reappear while we were there but the penguin soon came on to the ice again.[1]

The seals have apparently all pupped now and the young are growing quickly. We saw two males on the ice, and they showed the wonted laziness and good nature of the Weddell seal, never showing any resentment at being worried and proded with sticks. One of these males was at an old trap-hole, some 300 yards from the land, and near him was a dead black-throated penguin, picked almost clean by the gulls. The head was 100 yards from the body, and from the uninjured condition of the skeleton the penguin can hardly have been killed by the seal. Unless he met his death from disease, he must have been killed by the gulls, for the cold lately has not been nearly

---

[1] It seems improbable that Weddell seals ever prey on penguins.

severe enough to affect a penguin. Snowies, black-backed gulls and nellies seen in addition to the black-throated penguins.

Oct. 8th.—The birds seen were snowies, black-backed gulls and nellies, as well as many black-throated penguins. We killed twenty-three penguins at the Point Martin rookery for skins and food. A nelly swooped down and tore a piece from the breast of one of the killed, only a few yards from the cook. Courtship seemed to be beginning among the penguins; twice I saw two approach one another, and a mutual rubbing of beaks ensued to be followed by the one, probably the female, snapping at the other and moving off. No new seal pups to be seen. The same males seen as yesterday.

Oct. 9th.—The birds seen to-day were snowies, black-backed gulls and nellies, as well as a few adelia penguins coming from the south.

Oct. 10th.—The gentoo penguins have arrived. At the large penguin rookery at Point Martin [1] there were over 500 birds to-day of both species—adelia and gentoo, and at the nearer rookery by the " Half-moon " glacier there were also many penguins. I saw large bodies of them on their way to the big rookery from the open water, and as they arrived they clambered up on to the rocks at once. We met a flock of both species, some twenty or thirty of each, apparently mingling indiscriminately on their journey. As soon as we approached the adelias hurried on ahead of the gentoos, moving quickly on their bellies; when in front of us they stood up and stared, and with heads thrown upwards loudly screeched defiance, but on our further approach they turned tail and scattered away on their bellies for several hundred yards without stopping. Meanwhile the gentoos had been standing contemplating us quietly from further off, and when the retreating adelias passed them, they too fled, but in a more leisurely way, and always erect when possible, only flopping down when we came too near. The gentoos finally stopped far short of the more active adelias, and had resumed their course almost before the adelias had halted in their flight.

At the rookery nesting had begun and the birds seemed to be paired. The (?) male deliberately collected pebbles in his beak one by one, and dropped them in a small heap or a rough circle, while the (?) female meanwhile sat by and looked on. When I approached the male adelia screamed defiantly, while the female ran away; when she had got clear the male too retreated, but very unwillingly. We put two adelias in a seal hole, and in less than a minute they re-appeared with a sudden leap over two feet into the air, and, holding themselves in an erect position, they landed on the ice.

Two seals with fairly well developed pups were lying near the trap-hole. We drove them both in, but the youngsters would not follow. First one came out of the hole and moved towards the nearest youngster, but it turned out not to be hers, so she passed on to the other, and a mutual sniffing and rubbing of noses ensued, accompanied by various cries presumably indicative of joy. The rejected baby followed the adult, but when she saw it she turned and snarled at it as if warning it off, but made no attempt

[1] The largest rookeries in Scotia Bay were at Point Martin and along the coast and on the islets in the vicinity to north and south.

Zoological Log of Scottish National Antarctic Expedition.

[Photo by W. S. Bruce.

52. Blue-eyed Shag (*Phalacrocorax Atriceps*) on Nest at Rudmose Rocks,
South Orkneys.

[Photo by J. H. H. Pirie.

53. Gentoo Penguin (*Pygoscelis papua*) on Nest at Fergusile Peninsula,
South Orkneys.

[Photo by J. H. H. Pirie.

54. Ringed Penguins (*Pygoscelis Antarctica*) in Macdougall Bay,
South Orkneys.

[Photo by J. H. H. Pirie.

55. Ringed Penguins fighting at Point Thomson, Pirie Peninsula.

to injure it. The baby took the hint and moved away to await the return of its own mother. Three male seals at Point Martin.

In addition to the penguins, gulls, nellies and snowies were seen in plenty.

Oct. 11th.—The penguins were visited again to-day at their rookeries, and several stray ones moving northward were seen on the floe. At the near penguin rookery at the "Half-moon" glacier were about 120 penguins—gentoos and adelias in about equal numbers. At our approach they showed some alarm, but when they saw we did not intend to disturb them, the adelias resumed their work of nest-building. The gentoos, who were all on the lower part of the rookery and had not yet begun to build, showed much more fear and cleared out in a body at first, to return a little later, but with evident concern for their safety; and possibly serious doubts as to the desirability of the place for nesting. The adelias were nearly all actively collecting stones or resting from their labours, sleeping near their little heaps, either upright or prone. Some were very active and moved over ten yards at times in search of a good stone to return with; they throw the stones down in a heap in no apparent order. Thieving was being carried on extensively. The intending thief moved towards a heap the owner of which was away or not looking, and if he saw his chance picked up a stone and returned with it; but if the owner turned and spotted the thief approaching, the intending culprit walked innocently by as if nothing was further from his intentions than stealing a stone. If a thief was caught, the owner bit at him viciously and thus warned him off for the occasion, but as soon as an opportunity again presented itself he returned once more on thieving bent. I noticed several adelias eating snow in large quantities.

In addition, snowies, gulls and nellies were seen. The mate saw a paddy at Ailsa Craig.

Oct. 12th.—I visited the small penguin rookery and watched the birds at their work of stone-collecting, which was being actively pursued. Thieving was going on wholesale but never resulted in a fight; a vicious snarl was enough to frighten away the thief.

Mossman and the captain visited the large rookery and found hundreds of birds, chiefly black-throated, but as it was late in the day nearly all were roosting.

Gulls, nellies and snowies also seen. Young seals almost all taking the water.

Oct. 13th.—Snowies, black-backed gulls, nellies, gentoo and adelia penguins were seen. Johnnie Smith reports that three or four pairs of black-backed gulls have started nesting ashore opposite the ship, low down on the crags. The snowies also seem to be nesting by the noise and hubbub they are making, which they keep up all day and night. This afternoon some of us went out to the small penguin rookery for penguins, both for culinary and taxidermic purposes. There were only three pairs of gentoos, the weights and measurements of which were duly entered in the bird-book. They still seem to be at the nesting and stealing stage. They paid no heed to our slaughter except to help themselves to the stones of the ones which we slew.

Numerous bands of penguins cross from the rookery to the open water northwards

G

early in the morning, returning in small bands during the day. No skuas have put in an appearance yet, nor have we seen any shags near the ship, no doubt due to the lack of open water.

Oct. 14th.—This forenoon a party of us set out for the large penguin rookery to try and get some gentoo penguins. All available places are crowded with penguins, chiefly adelias, only to be numbered by thousands, and as high up as 150 feet above high-water mark. The penguins are still arriving at the rookery in a steady stream, and all the small islets are covered with them. We got two black-throated ones, and seventeen gentoos. There were very few gentoos, but they seemed to have paired off and settled on the rookery. One of the adelias was an immature bird, the throat not yet being black below the gonys, except for a few feathers. Most of them have their nests built, and are engaged in pilfering. Some were treading. While I was killing a black-throated penguin, its mate made a gallant sortie from the nest and attacked me, and was only driven off after many brave but fruitless charges on my sea-boots. While sledging the dead, or apparently dead, up to the ship, one of them, a gentoo, got up and scuttled away.

Snowies, nellies and black-backed gulls. No sign of skuas yet. There are several paddies scattered throughout the penguins, but they apparently are not yet " married."

Only a few seals seem now to be staying with their mothers ; most have " shoved off on their own."

Oct. 15th.—Snowies and a nelly are reported by Mossman. Nobody has been out at the rookeries. Zoologically it has been a very quiet day.

Oct. 16th.—Went out to the penguin rookeries on the west side of the bay to see if we could get any eggs ; the birds had not commenced to lay. On the way back saw two Weddell seals, both males, fast asleep on the ice. Several snowy petrels, black-backed gulls and nellies were seen.

Oct. 17th.—A misty day ; remained on board all day. Did not see any birds ; heard some snowy petrels about the cliffs.

Oct. 19th.—A party, consisting of Brown, Pirie and several others, went out to the penguin rookery to get some penguins for phonographic records. Brown says that as usual, the gentoos, on the approach of the party, were much alarmed, and a body of them left the rookery, whilst the adelias, on the other hand, stayed and showed no concern, unless one walked amongst them, when they did not run, but shrieked defiance. The gentoo's courtship, Brown describes as being very similar to that of the adelia, but in this, as in all their other actions, they are less energetic. When braying, the gentoos assume the same position as an emperor penguin, namely, they stand erect with their heads well back, beaks pointing upwards, and flippers stretched from their sides. Their cry, as that of the emperor, somewhat resembles the bray of a donkey. The gentoo sometimes assumes the same attitude, and apparently indulges in a deep yawn without emitting any sound. The adelias have not yet been observed to have this habit.

When the penguins were being put into a crate, they distinctly caught hold of the bars with their flippers, which they entwined half round them for some moments ; some of them thus held on, supporting the whole weight of their bodies on their flippers. I saw a skua, the first one, I believe, seen this season in Scotia Bay. Pirie saw a black-backed gull's nest, consisting chiefly of earthy matter, built within easy distance of the cliffs.

Snowy petrels, nellies and paddies were also observed. A seal was seen in Uruguay Cove by Mr Bruce.

Oct. 20th.—Usual birds about. Nothing fresh zoologically.

Oct. 21st.—Mr Bruce and Kerr paid a visit to the penguin rookery to take a cinematograph view of the birds. Brown came back from a walk with a dead Wilson's petrel, and Pirie with a baby seal's skull, which he found near Delta Island. He reports having seen the white gull, and also terns, which he thought he heard two or three days ago for the first time this season. The captain saw a skua. Several snowies, nellies, including a white one, and black-backed gulls about. Two Weddell seals are reported to have been seen on the floe near Delta Island, a male and female together, court-ing ; the male appeared to be bitten in several places. Many seals were also seen by Pirie off Delta Island, also some black-backed gulls' nests near Point Davis which were made of earthy matter, lichens and mosses, penguin feathers and limpet shells.

Oct. 22nd.—Davidson went with a party to secure two seals for museum specimens. They got a couple of Weddell seals off Delta Island, a male and a female, and saw many others. The male was of no use for a skin, as it was badly scarred, besides having its lower jaw broken. The males are evidently fighting amongst themselves, and this appears to be their rutting season. A female with its young was also secured in Uruguay Cove. A tern, snowies, black-backed gulls, nellies and penguins were also seen.

Oct. 23rd.—Cape pigeons, snowies, black-backed gulls, a skua and nellies were seen about the ship. The latter flew quite close to the ship, and alighted on the midden-heap, where there is some seal's blubber and meat. They also damaged a very handsomely marked skin of a young Weddell seal, which Pirie had shot in Uruguay Cove, by picking off the skin about the eyes.

Oct. 24th.—Brown went to the near penguin rookery to look for eggs ; he did not find any, however, though a careful search was made. The young seal which was captured two days ago has escaped. Paddies, skuas, black-backed gulls and nellies have been reported to-day.

Oct. 25th.—A skua and two paddies were shot to-day. Black-backed gulls and nellies have also been seen. Murray said that he saw Cape pigeons' nests on the cliffs on the North Beach.

Oct. 26th.—Two terns were shot by Pirie off Point Davis. About six skuas, as well as several gulls and nellies, were seen. Paddies have returned to the ship ; they are also present amongst the penguins on the rookeries. No penguins' eggs yet.

Brown found the gentoos nesting; their nests are larger than those of the adelias, and they not only contain more stones, but also old tail feathers and a few bones. The adelias were seen scooping out holes in their stone heaps, as if preparatory to laying.

Oct. 27th.—Paddies, nellies, black-backed gulls, snowy petrels, skuas and black-throated penguins have been seen. No one has been out much, and these birds were seen from the ship and the house on shore.

Oct. 28th.—Mr Bruce paid a visit to the nearer penguin rookery; no eggs yet. The gentoos were also nesting there. He also saw a gull's nest. Nellies, including a white one, black-backed gulls, snowy petrels and paddies have been seen. A batch of penguins was observed on the floe near to the house. Pirie described the tern's nest as being mostly composed of limpet shells.

Mr Bruce and I each shot a skua.

Oct. 29th.—Mr Bruce got the first (black-throated) penguin's egg this morning from the small penguin rookery, and about a dozen were got in the afternoon by Brown and Pirie from the other rookeries. These are the first eggs that the penguins have laid, and they were only to be secured after a careful search through the rookeries. A Cape pigeon, paddies, penguins, black-backed gulls, nellies and snowy petrels were seen during the day. A batch of about twenty penguins was seen moving towards the North Beach about 4.30 P.M., all going in Indian file, and paddling along the snow on their breasts and bellies, by means of their feet and flippers.

Davidson shot three seals, one female and two males, about two months old, all Weddells.

Brown found several specimens of a small acarinid among the moss on the slopes of Mossman Peninsula.

Oct. 30th.—A number of eggs were secured from the penguin rookeries. Usual birds seen.

Oct. 31st. 1903.[1]—This morning 709 eggs of the adelia penguin were gathered at the large penguin rookery, but the majority of birds have not laid yet.

In four cases I saw two eggs in a nest, and a like number was seen in three other nests. Most of the eggs were very dirty; generally speaking, only the new-laid ones are clean. As a rule, the birds lie down on their eggs and defend them valiantly, but some more timid ones retreat and leave their eggs to their fate. Skuas were seen hovering incessantly over the rookery, about three to ten feet above the birds, or at times sitting still on some high position or outstanding rock near by. The penguins scream defiantly when the skuas approach too near. I saw a skua making off with a whole egg in his mouth, and he refused to drop it, even on my chasing him, before he took to wing. The gentoos have not yet laid, and are as timid as ever. Paddies also seen about the rookery.

In the afternoon, Johnnie Smith brought in a penguin whose leg had been broken

---

[1] During the absence of D. W. Wilton on a sledge expedition this log was kept by R. N. Rudmose Brown until Nov. 26th.

Zoological Log of Scottish National Antarctic Expedition.

[*Photo by W. S. Bruce.*

56. Ringed Penguins (*Pygoscelis Antarctica*) Courting.   Point Thomson, South Orkneys.

[*Photo by D. W. Wilton.*

57. Ringed Penguins Mating.   Point Thomson, South Orkneys.

and had set again in a curious fashion, with the useless foot turned lower side upmost
attached to the side of the leg. A shag was also caught at the open water near
Point Martin, and it disgorged some small fish when struck. Mackenzie killed a skua
with a stick in the afternoon.

Nov. 1st.—A southerly gale. Skuas, paddies and penguins seen. Three paddies
shot. Gulls and snowy petrels wheel incessantly about the cliffs, the latter, as a rule,
high up. Bodies of penguins, both adelia and gentoo, pass between the rookeries and
their feeding grounds in Jessie Bay, and nellies and skuas pass by occasionally,
the nellies still attracted by blubber and carrion, but the skuas more intent on hovering
over penguin rookeries in search of eggs. About 3000 eggs (actual total 3145) brought
in to-day from the large rookery by all hands. Several nests with two eggs in each.
A shag and a tern seen over Jessie Bay in the afternoon. One gentoo egg was found
at the large rookery, but so near in appearance do they approach to the adelia eggs,
that, being put in the same basket, it was impossible to definitely pick it out when the
eggs came aboard.

Johnnie Smith saw a ringed penguin (*Pygoscelis antarctica*) at the big rookery
to-day.

Nov. 3rd.—The penguins appear to leave the rookeries in the early morning and
move to the open water, returning about noon and all through the afternoon. A great
many gentoos passed the house, travelling south this morning; by their numbers they
would appear to be new arrivals.

Snowy petrels are circling about high up on the face of the cliffs. Skuas and
black-backed gulls are to be seen around the ship and the house whenever there is any
carrion. There was also a white nelly this morning by the house. A large flock
of several hundred shags flew northward. At Point Davis I saw many gulls either
wheeling overhead or settling in pairs on the snow. Terns were also pairing, but
I found no nests.

A Weddell seal in Uruguay Cove.

Nov. 4th.—The birds seen were adelia and gentoo penguins, but fewer, since
Jessie Bay and Uruguay Cove are very full of ice. Nellies, skuas, terns, gulls, paddies
and snowies. Skuas are becoming very numerous.

Nov. 5th.—Jessie Bay and Uruguay Cove open again, and several bodies of penguins
crossed over from the rookeries in the morning, and returned in the afternoon.

I went to the small rookery[1] in the afternoon and marked several eggs, which
appeared new-laid, with the date. More gentoos have arrived there, and occupied
some of the low-lying ground. As usual, they ran when I came near them, but
returned as soon as I had passed; in the meantime I had put an adelia egg in a gentoo
nest. The owner of the nest returned, and looked at the egg suspiciously, sniffed it

[1] This small rookery, the nearest to the ship, is on a rocky islet, off the " Half-moon " glacier, named
Theodolite Point. On Nov. 8th all eggs were cleared away, and, after that date, eggs were marked daily,
and embryos taken with a view to obtaining a complete series for a study of the development of the
gentoo penguin.

several times, and ultimately sat beside the nest, not on it. A skua, who swooped down to pick up the egg, was evidently recognised as an enemy under any conditions, and all the birds near combined in frightening him away.

No gentoo eggs are yet to be found at the small rookery. This rookery is now preserved, and no one is allowed to kill birds or to gather eggs there. Skuas, gulls, snowy petrels and nellies seen to-day. Cape pigeons at their nests at the south-west corner of the North Beach.

Ten skuas shot near the house in the evening where they come to feed on penguin "crans" and other carrion.

Nov. 6th.—Skuas very common around the house. Gulls and paddies also, feeding on what they could find. A large light-grey nelly was shot on The Beach. A flock of shags flew northward about 5 A.M. All hands were at the large penguin rookery this afternoon, and brought back 2140 adelia eggs, and 36 gentoo eggs. The eggs of the gentoo are, on the whole, whiter and more round than those of the adelia, yet, so alike are the two, that it is very difficult to distinguish them. Gentoos only lay one egg in a nest.[1] Three were found in one adelia nest. Very few penguins went to Uruguay Cove this morning. Mossman saw a flock of gentoos arrive at the edge of the bay from the south. On finding the bay full of ice, they gave expression to their disappointment in several loud brays, and then returned. The returning party met a small flock on their way north; both stopped for a seeming interchange of compliments, and then went on their way. I saw the same thing later on, but two of the returning gentoos deserted their comrades, and joined the flock moving north.

Nov. 7th.—Skuas very plentiful, both near the house and ship, as well as at the rookery. Gulls, snowy petrels, paddies and terns also seen, and one nelly.

Four specimens of the ringed penguin secured to-day; one pair is said to have taken their place on the big rookery and several others have been seen on the floe, but, as yet, they have not come in any great numbers.

The gentoo eggs are most characteristic as regards their yolk, which is a rich orange-red, almost a vermilion.

A flock of shags passed north early this morning.

Nov. 8th.—Snowy petrels and gulls about the cliffs. Cape pigeons on their nests, but no eggs yet. Skuas very plentiful, two terns, and a nelly, also some paddies at the rookery. Six ringed penguins on the North Beach early this morning, and one at the big rookery.

The North Beach was clear all day, but comparatively few penguins left the rookeries to fish. Most of these who did pass were gentoos, who are not yet so busy with their eggs as the adelias are. Gravill and I went to the small rookery in the afternoon and cleared all the eggs away from the easternmost rocks of it, and also all the gentoo eggs in the rookery. The gentoo eggs from the big rookery were all taken this morning. At the small rookery, where the penguins have been left undisturbed for

[1] The gentoos frequently only lay one egg, though often two, but never three.

some time, practically every nest has two eggs now; this seems to be the normal number laid.

Nov. 9th.—Ringed penguins are becoming more plentiful, and about ten were killed in the evening. Mossman saw three in the morning on the North Beach, who did not appear in the least afraid of him, until some terrified gentoos passed them, which seemed to create a panic among the ringed, who at once joined the gentoos in their flight. I met a ringed on The Beach in the forenoon, and he seemed even more courageous than the adelias, for, not content with facing me defiantly, he charged me, and began a determined attack on my legs. This performance he repeated several times, after I had worried him with a stick on each occasion. Ultimately a harder blow sent him scuttling off on his belly. The ringed appear to be far more reluctant to travel in this position than the adelias, and, unlike the adelias, they propel themselves with both flippers simultaneously and not alternately. I visited the small rookeries, and marked with the date these eggs laid since yesterday in the restricted area. An adelia egg which I put in a gentoo nest the other day was cold, and the gentoo sat beside it and refused to sit on it. To-day (Nov. 9th) the gentoo is sitting on it.

Skuas plentiful, two grey nellies near the house, a small flock of shags over Jessie Bay, many gulls and snowy petrels. The Cape pigeons have not laid yet. Paddies also seen.

The small trap on the port bow which has been down about a month was taken up to-day and contained 89 cushion-stars and one fish of the ordinary kind (14 ounces, 12½ inches).

Nov. 10th.—Skuas, nellies and gulls seen. Terns at Point Davis. I visited the small rookery and marked the new-laid eggs in the reserved area. Some of the gentoos are becoming quite courageous, and in several cases I had forcibly to remove the bird from its nest before I could get at the egg. One gentoo nest had two eggs. All hands were at the big rookery collecting eggs—1950 adelia, 134 gentoo. They saw one pair of ringed penguins there, but no gentoos. The captain was at Delta Island and saw about 100 ringed penguins there, but no gentoos. Very few penguins on The Beach or floe to-day. North-west wind, and Jessie Bay full of ice.

Many seals of about two months and a few adults at Delta Island, all of them Weddells.

Nov. 11th.—Very few penguins passed the ship but I saw numbers of them going to the open water to the south. A few ringed on the big rookery. I visited the small rookery and marked eggs; the skuas have been making a raid on the gentoo eggs in one part of the rookery as there were fewer there than yesterday. Some of the gentoos are becoming quite courageous; one even offered to bite me—a most unusual proceeding for the gentoo. Skuas plentiful; two shot near the house and a half-blind one captured alive near the ship. He was tame enough on deck, but his blindness may account for that. Gulls much less common of late—they must be nesting. Two nellies and a few paddies seen. Snowies circling around high up on the cliffs, giving vent continually to their "kaa-kaa." Cape pigeons have not yet laid. A dark stormy petrel was seen to-day both near the ship and up the glacier. It was very like Wilson's petrel *(Oceanites oceanicus).*

Wilton and Macdougall, who came in from the camp[1] to fetch a few things, brought stories of countless shags' eggs, of huge nellies' eggs, and of Cape pigeons nesting in legion.

Nov. 12th.—North-westerly wind and driving snow. No penguins observed on the floe, but numbers could be seen from aloft going to the open water to the south, which is gradually getting nearer. Skuas more numerous than ever. Many of them, when sitting around their carrion feast, indulge in a curious habit; they open their wings backward to their full extent until they touch at the tips but make no attempt to fly; for some seconds they keep them in this position giving vent at same time to their shrill cry of "keh-keh!" They then lower them and continue their meal. At times this seems to be done with intent to scare away an intruding skua but it may on the other hand be related to sexual selection.

One nelly seen coming from the north; nellies are now scarce for they are busy breeding. (The boat party have found two breeding-places in Brown's Bay.)

One or two gulls seen and some snowy petrels.

Nov. 13th.—Blowing from W.N.W. with snow. I visited the small rookery and marked the new eggs except these which were too dirty to write on, and which I brought back—all gentoos. Gentoo eggs of 9th and 10th have all got a second egg laid beside the first. (NOTE.—Eggs dated 13th may be 12th or 13th, as I could not visit the rookery yesterday.) The gentoos are getting less timid.

A few penguins going to the water in the south but none going to the north. Skuas about the ship in numbers. A few gulls seen.

Johnnie Smith was out at the camp at Point Thomson and brought in a nelly's egg and six shags' eggs. The nelly's egg is 10·3 inches by 6·5 inches, and 8½ ounces.

Three seals, one at least an adult, just beyond the big penguin rookery.

Nov. 14th.—Snow all day and very misty. Skuas at the carrion heap, also black-backed gulls and three nellies. Snowy petrels and paddies seen about the rookery. About 100 ringed penguins are nesting on the big rookery but none on the small one. Many penguins going to the water in the south to feed. I marked eggs at the small rookery as usual. Nests where first egg was laid on the 11th have now a second egg. I found one gentoo egg entirely without a shell but the bird sat on it like an ordinary egg. To-day the adelias were continually shaking themselves of the snow and wet on their coats, and their way of doing it is exactly like a dog's. About 100 ringed penguins were found nesting on the big rookery scattered here and there among the others. 200 gentoo eggs and three terns' eggs were brought back from a nest a little beyond the rookery. The tern's egg is olive green with irregular grey and brown spots all over it. Tern's egg 1·3 inches by 1·7 inches. Weight, 0·9 ounces.

[1] This camp was on Point Thomson in Brown's Bay.

Zoological Log of Scottish National Antarctic Expedition.

[Photo by R. C. Mossman.

58. Antarctic Skuas (*Megalestris antarcticus*) Fighting on The Beach,
Scotia Bay.

[Photo by W. S. Bruce.

59. Antarctic Skua Flying, MacDougall Bay, South Orkneys.

[Photo by J. H. H. Pirie.

60. Antarctic Skua on Nest, Mossman Peninsula, South Orkneys.

[Photo by J. H. H. Pirie.

61. The White-rumped Tern (*Sterna hirundinacea*) at Point Davis, S. Orkneys.

Nov. 15th.—I marked the new-laid eggs at the small rookery. Eggs of the 11th have all a second one beside them now; a few of the 13th also have. One gentoo is sitting on four eggs, two of which I put into its nest.

The skuas are playing great havoc, particularly among the gentoos, and many nests have lost eggs since yesterday. Jessie Bay and Uruguay Cove are open again, and many penguins are travelling to and fro between the water and the small rookery. A few ringed penguins about the floe. Three more terns' eggs were obtained near the big rookery, and I got two gulls' eggs at Point Davis. The gulls' nests are of lichen and moss on any flat open rock; none of them were more than twenty feet above sea-level. The egg is very like the tern's in colour and shape but browner, and some three to four times as large. There was one egg in each nest. The gulls flew away on my approach and settled on a near snow-hill until I left. (NOTE.—Eggs were probably obtained there yesterday by a member of the crew, which makes the date of gull's first laying not later than Nov. 14th.) Terns are building at the same point, but have not laid yet. Gull's egg, 3 inches by 1·9 inches, and 3 ounces in weight.

Skuas very numerous, particularly near the ship and on the North Beach. A few nellies also seen. Terns, snowies and paddies.

Pirie found a paddy's nest near the big rookery, but no eggs. There are also Cape pigeons nesting there as well as a pair of Wilson's petrels. Several young seals near the big rookery and two adults at Point Davis. Two much scarred adult *Lobodons* seen near the big rookery.

Nov. 16th.—A nelly shot at the house and several others seen during the day. Over twenty skuas at the ship and about eight black-backed gulls as well as several paddies. Terns and snowy petrels also seen. Adelia, gentoo and ringed penguins on the floe, particularly gentoo. I visited the small rookery as usual. Many of the gentoo nests are almost snowed up except for the space kept clear by the heat of the bird's body. Two or three nests more exposed than the others are completely snowed up, and the gentoos belonging to them are homeless.

The sledge sent to the camp with provisions this morning returned with Cape pigeons, snowy petrels and ringed penguins for skeletons, and some specimens from Macdougall Bay and Brown's Bay, including a compound ascidian and a small crab.

Nov. 17th.—Skuas in numbers, a few nellies and gulls, and three or four paddies about the ship. A few terns seen. Got two terns' eggs beyond the big rookery and also a gull's egg which, however, was unfortunately broken. I visited the small rookery and marked the new-laid eggs. Birds who laid their first egg on the 13th, and most of those who did so on the 14th, have now a second egg. Many empty egg-shells lying about tell the story of the skuas' raids. At the big rookery I saw a skua swoop down within three feet of me and seize an uncovered egg and fly off with it. He settled down some twenty yards off, put down the egg, cracked it with a bite and sucked out the contents. Meantime a second skua, probably his mate, sat by and looked on as if waiting her chance for a taste. Paddies too seen in various places on

H

the rookery sitting on prominent rocks, doubtless on the look-out for dead penguins or broken eggs. Several of these paddies allowed me to get within six feet of them without showing any concern, and even then they only walked away; they seemed to be very unwilling to fly. One paddy would only run when I had shoved him with my stick. Several penguins of all three kinds seen travelling on the floe at different times of the day.

A dead baby seal was found beyond the big rookery, probably two or three days old. Its brain especially had been eaten by nellies.

Nov. 18th.—Jessie Bay and Uruguay Cove open again with a southerly wind, and many penguins on the floe. In the main, they seem to go to the water in the early morning and return in evening, but parties of them come and go in addition at all times of the day. Stragglers and couples are often to be seen, but more generally they travel in flocks of six or eight, or thirty or forty, and these flocks may be all of one species, or two or even three species will be found together. At the small rookery the nests which have a new-laid egg had their first egg on the 15th. The gentoos are daily becoming more courageous, and every day a larger number have to be removed from their nests to enable me to get at their eggs.

I noticed a ringed penguin to-night, when pursued by the cook, moving along by a series of short quick jumps instead of scuttling on its belly, as is their more usual custom.

The usual skuas, gulls, snowies, paddies and terns were seen, and also one nelly. No nests, other than penguins', were visited.

Nov. 19th.—Skuas and gulls about the ship but not in such great numbers as usual. A few paddies at the ship and more at the rookery. At Point Davis, I got eight gulls' eggs and three terns' eggs. The gulls' eggs were found, three in one nest, two each in two nests and one in another nest. The gulls flew away and left their nests as I approached. The terns build no nest but lay their solitary egg on any flat earthy crevice in the rocks; others lay among limpet-shells, which must be brought there by birds in summer. The terns also flew away, but betrayed the whereabouts of their egg by hovering in the air uttering a loud scream. At the big rookery the ringed penguins have not yet laid, and the other birds' nests were not visited. At the small rookery nests of 16th have now a second egg, and a few nests have three eggs, in which case an interval of only two days seems as a rule to elapse between the third and second egg.

Nov. 20th.—Skuas, gulls and two nellies at the ship. Cape pigeons at Uruguay Cove. Many skuas at the house wrangling over penguin carcases. They allow one within ten to twenty feet without showing any alarm. Also a number of skuas resting on the North Beach and others bathing off floes. At the small rookery all eggs of the 16th, and a large number of the 17th, have now a second egg. The skuas do not seem to get many eggs from the adelias, but on the other hand, the loss of eggs among the gentoos, particularly the outlying ones, is great.

I saw one ringed penguin wandering through the small rookery as if in search of a nesting-place. When attacked by the sitting penguins he moved rapidly by a series of short quick jumps.

To-day I noticed that the great majority of penguins on the rookery have developed a featherless tract of skin over the belly lying medianly. It runs 3 or 4 inches up from the base of the white coat, and is about 1 to 1½ inches broad. The violet coloured skin shows distinctly. When the bird is lying on its eggs, they are covered by this groove in its feather coat, so that above they lie against the bare skin, and on either side are surrounded by the feathers. Both gentoos and adelias show this adaptation for keeping the eggs warm. I noticed a single case of it some two weeks ago, and others have occasionally been noted lately, but to-day is the first day it has become quite generally visible among the penguins.

Nov. 21*st.*—At the small rookery eggs of the 18th have generally a companion now, but on the whole few eggs are being laid. A pair of ringed penguins are evidently going to settle there. On the moss-covered slopes of the land beyond, skuas are settling down in pairs, and courtship is proceeding merrily. They allow one within a few feet of them without showing any concern.

At the big rookery the ringed penguins have not yet laid. One tern's egg was got further along the bay. Duncan and Anderson report having seen a large penguin, three times the size of an adelia, but similar in colour, except for its black feet and gentoo-like shaped bill. It escaped into the water before they could capture it. Its size they compared with several adelias near by. Accounts given to me by each of the men separately are quite consistent.[1]

Skuas, a few gulls, a nelly and some snowy petrels also seen. One skua found dead on the floe between the ship and the shore.

Nov. 22*nd.*—Rookeries not visited to-day. Gulls, skuas, paddies, a nelly or two, and a tern, as well as three Wilson's petrels seen.

Nov. 23*rd.*—Scotia Bay has broken up and the ship is free again. Before the ice broke up, three adult Weddell seals were shot near the rookery and brought in for skeletons—one female and two males. Several other seals were seen when the ice went out. The break-up of the bay was accompanied by the arrival of many birds; penguins were disporting themselves in the water; terns and snowy petrels were plentiful; skuas and nellies settled on the cook's midden, and on various scraps of blubber as they floated off on the ice-floes. Wilson's petrels were numerous. Paddies also seen. The Cape pigeons nesting at The Beach have lately deserted their nests, but no eggs have been laid.

A compound ascidian was seen in the water to-day. The trap off the port bow was raised finally this afternoon, and contained twenty fish of the usual kind, sixty-eight cushion-stars, and two yellow star-fish.

Nov. 24*th.*[2]—Shags have settled on the small rocky islet west of the ship, and are

---

[1] There is little doubt that this was an immature emperor penguin which had wandered far north.

[2] The *Scotia* left Scotia Bay *via* Washington Strait (to the west) for the encampment at Point Thomson, Brown's Bay. She returned to Scotia Bay at night.

flying about over the water. Terns, snowy petrels, skuas and nellies are also to be seen, the first in large numbers. Penguins and seals in the water.

Several large penguin rookeries seen round the coast in Washington Strait and at Nigg Rock. In Brown's Bay there is a rookery of ringed penguins. Cape pigeons plentiful about the ship when in Brown's Bay, and several Wilson's petrels also seen there. Weddell seals seen in Scotia Bay.

Nov. 25th, At anchor in Scotia Bay.—Nellies, skuas, shags, terns, paddies, snowies and gulls seen to-day. Many shags settling on the water fishing. Twenty-three of them were shot, and one, on being hauled on board, disgorged a fish, 10 inches long, of the rarer green species. Many gentoos in the water; they do not leap so far out of the water as the adelias do, and are much more fond of sitting on the surface.

A compound ascidian caught on the surface, and a common cushion-star on a fishing line.

Nov. 26th,[1] North Coast and Jessie Bay.—Same birds seen as yesterday, and many Cape pigeons in addition.

Nov. 27th.—Started early this morning for the Falkland Islands. Mr Bruce landed at Eillium Island off Jessie Bay, and secured thirty eggs of the ringed penguins; these are similar to the black-throated and gentoo penguins' eggs. When off Coronation Island a few grampuses were sighted. Silver petrels, Cape pigeons, terns, nellies and some blue petrels were also seen.

Nov. 28th, 59° 43′ S. 48° 10′ W.—Bottle-noses and finners were conspicuous during the day. In the morning saw several ringed penguins in the water. Cape pigeons, terns, nellies, silver petrels and some blue petrels[2] were also seen, the latter only towards evening. A piece of a siphonophore tentacle was caught on the sounding line at 210 fathoms, but came up rather broken. Saw a *Doliolum* floating past. Hooked a piece of rotten kelp which was full of barnacles, some of which we bottled.

Nov. 29th, 58° 28′ S. 51° 56′ W.—Many finners were seen early this morning. Whilst sounding, three Cape pigeons were caught. Tried to secure a sooty albatros, but failed. Tow-nettings have been taken by Brown; no animals have been found in them as yet. A Cape hen was seen for the first time since we were in these latitudes last, sooty albatroses, molliemauks, blue petrels and Cape pigeons in plenty. In the evening saw two or three Wilson's petrels.

Nov. 30th, 57° 10′ S. 55° 35′ W.—A few Cape hens were seen early this morning, also a few molliemauks and sooty albatroses. Blue petrels and Cape pigeons in plenty. No whales were seen. Mr Bruce saw a sooty albatros with the characteristic head and eye, but white underneath like a mollie.[3] Some penguins were seen by the captain.

Dec. 1st, 54° 55′ S. 57° 28′ W.—Three albatroses, appearing to be intermediate between the sooty albatros and molliemauk, were secured during the day. A painting

---

[1] The *Scotia* left for Brown's Bay *via* Washington Strait, and anchored for the night in Uruguay Cove.
[2] These proved to be *Prion banski*.   [3] This was probably *Phoebetria cornicoides*.

Zoological Log of Scottish National Antarctic Expedition.

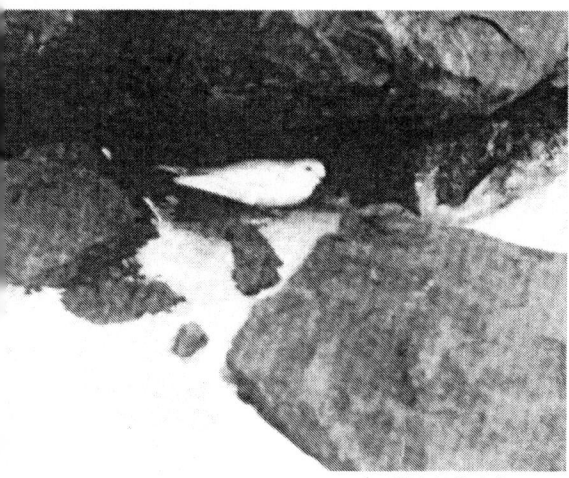

[Photo by W. S. Bruce.

Snowy Petrel (*Pagodroma nivea*) on Nest, Jessie Bay, South Orkneys.

[Photo by W. S. Bruce.

63. Snowy Petrel flying, Weddell Sea. The snowy petrel indicates the proximity of pack ice.

[Photo by J. H. H. Pirie.

64. Young Southern Great Black-backed or Dominican Gulls (*Larus dominicanus*) in down.

[Photo by W. S. Bruce.

65. Cape Pigeons (*Daption capensis*) preparing to Nest, MacDougall Bay, Ferguslie Peninsula.

of the beak of one of them was made by Mr Bruce; they differ in colour especially about the head, some being much lighter in colour than the others. The bills also differ in colour, the three we secured yesterday showing this. Two of them have a yellow culmen, and yellow under the lower mandible, while the third is almost entirely grey. The inside of the mouth is yellow; the legs are of a pale grey, almost white in parts, mottled with the darker grey towards the outer ends of the webs. The grey has a distinct lavender tinge about it, much the same as the feathers. The eye-lid is black as well as the cere; at the lower angle posteriorly is a white patch of feathers, which in flight looks like a white eyelid. The eye has a dark olive-green iris, while the pupil is bluish-black. (This has been painted.) The remains of a crustacean, about the size of a Norway lobster, were found in the stomach of one of the birds above mentioned.

Blue petrels, Cape pigeons, molliemauks, sooty albatroses, a wandering albatros, Wilson's petrels and penguins were seen.

In the evening a trawl was let down on the Burdwood Bank in 56 fathoms, and dragged over the bottom for forty minutes. The dynomometer registered a little over 4 tons, and about 150 fathoms of steel wire rope were paid out. Unfortunately just before heaving up, the iron bolt (" goose-neck "), which fixes the derrick on to the main-mast gave way, and caused considerable delay in hauling up the trawl; in consequence we had to sort the catch by lamp-light.

The catch was an excellent one, and everyone on board was interested in sorting it, which took us till two o'clock on the following morning, for the greater part, and till noon on Tuesday before everything was bottled.[1] There was a great abundance of sponges, and a kind of bryozoa. As we sorted the material out in comparative darkness, phosphorescence was observed in some of the fishes, bryozoa, sponges, alcyonarians, and in one large crab.

About seventy species were included in the catch, of which the following is a rough list.

Fish.—Four species represented by eleven, nineteen, one, and one specimens respectively.

Ascidians	3 species.	Ophiuroids	4 species.
Gasteropods	4 ,,	Asteroids	5 or 6 species.
Lamellibranchs	3 ,,	Crinoids	3 ,,
Chiton	1 ,,	Holothurians	2 ,,
Brachiopod	1 ,,	Bryozoa	7 ,,
Crabs	5 or 6 species.	Alcyonarians	3 ,,
Shrimp	1 ,,	Sponges	5 or 6 ,,
Barnacle	1 ,,	Pennatulids	2 ,,
Polychaetes	5 or 6 ,,	Other coelenterates	1 ,,
Echinoids	2 ,,	and various other species.

Brown got some crustaceans in his tow-netting before the trawl. Position of trawl 54° 25′ S. 57° 32′ W.

[1] The largest and richest catch of the Expedition, totalling about half a ton.

Dec. 2nd, 52° 11' S. 57° 55' W.—Shags, Cape pigeons, young and old black-backed gulls, sooty albatroses and some penguins were seen during the day. Could not make out what species the penguins were as they did not stay any length of time above water.

Dec. 2nd to 9th, Port Stanley, Falkland Islands.—Did not have much opportunity of making any excursions. Brown and I went for a stroll one evening, and saw a crimson-breasted bird like a dotterel, with its mate, which had no crimson on it.[1] On Sunday morning, Mr Bruce and I went for a stroll eastwards, and saw the following birds—black-backed gulls, nellies, skuas, steamer-ducks,[2] some with families, a kind of tringa and a hawk. On Dec. 9th we left Port Stanley at 6 A.M. Could not lift the trap, which we had left on entering Port William, owing to stress of weather. Sooty albatroses, molliemauks, Wilson's and blue petrels, also nellies were seen during the day.

Dec. 10th, 48° 22' S. 56° 49' W.—Same birds seen as yesterday, also a wandering albatros, and a sperm whale. Sea phosphorescent at night.

Dec. 11th, 46° 14' S. 56° 10' W.—Three albatroses, a molliemauk, several Wilson's petrels, and three birds, which were flying too far off to distinguish the species, probably prion petrels. Sea very phosphorescent at night.

Dec. 12th, 44° 08' S. 57° 30' W.—Albatroses, molliemauks, Wilson's and prion petrels seen. A school of porpoises was also observed. Davidson saw a whale. Sea very phosphorescent at night.

Dec. 13th, 42° 30' S. 59° 18' W.—Wandering albatroses and molliemauks. Prion petrels and Wilson's petrels have been seen during the day, though not in large numbers.

Dec. 14th, 40° 32' S. 58° 33' W.—Molliemauks and Wilson's petrels seen. A large flock of birds settling on the water was observed in the afternoon : under wing and belly white, the upper surface of the wing and the back apparently dark brown. Could not make them out, as I did not see them close enough to get a good view. The luminosity of the sea is very marked to-night.

Dec. 15th, Off Cape Corrientes, 38° 24' S. 57° 42' W.—The birds described yesterday are probably shear-waters (*Puffinus gravis*, the great shear-water).

A whole flock of these birds were seen settling, and flying immediately above a shoal of mackerel. Some albatroses, molliemauks and Wilson's petrels seen.

Dec. 16th, Off Cape Corrientes.—Shear-waters, molliemauks and Wilson's petrels seen, also porpoises.

Dec. 17th, Off Cape Corrientes.—Same kind of birds, mammals and fish as yesterday. Saw a small bird and judged it to be a tern from its flight.

Dec. 18th, Off Cape Corrientes.—Very few birds seen to-day, probably owing to hazy and rainy weather ; two or three shear-waters. Two seals were seen quite close to the ship ; they did not remain near. Brown saw a fin of a sun-fish. Several schools of porpoises were playing around the ship. Flies were observed on the poop in the

---

[1] *Trupialis militaris.*   [2] *Tachyeres cinereus.*

afternoon. A good deal of phosphorescence has been observed at nights since the 14th inst.

Dec. 19th, Off Cape Corrientes.—A flock of terns were seen towards the evening; they looked from afar very much like the terns seen in Scotia Bay. I saw several of them swooping down into the water, and rising almost immediately afterwards. A seal was also seen in the morning, as well as a large school of porpoises. Flies are getting quite numerous. Three moths have been seen, and, though two were captured, they managed to escape. A small beetle, with yellow longitudinal lines on the back, was caught. Brown saw two mosquitoes. Phosphorescence not so marked.

Dec. 20th, Off Medano Point.—No birds seen to-day, except a flock of land-birds reported in the morning, but too far off to make out. Some moths and beetles were captured. Did not observe any phosphorescence at night.

Dec. 21st, Rio de la Plata.—A few small land birds were seen. Many moths, several dragon-flies, lady-birds and beetles were observed.

Dec. 22nd, Ortiz Bank, Rio de la Plata.—Same beasts as yesterday. Could not make the birds out.

Dec. 23rd.—Dropped anchor at Outer Roads of Buenos Aires at 2 P.M.

*   *   *   *   *   *   *   *   *   *

Jan. 21st, 1904.—Left Buenos Aires on our second Antarctic voyage.

Jan. 22nd, 35° 11′ S. 57° 01′ W.—Cleared the Rio de la Plata.

Jan. 23rd, 36° 57′ S. 55° 45′ W.—An albatros and some petrels, probably prions, were seen, also a school of fish, probably mackerel. Sea very luminous during the night.

Jan. 24th, 39° 24′ S. 55° 02′ W.—Prion petrels, a school of porpoises, and a seal are the animals seen to-day. The flies in the cabin are thinning out. Sea very luminous at night.

Jan. 25th, 40° 59′ S. 55° 04′ W.—Prion petrels were very plentiful. A *Velella* was caught in the draw-bucket and bottled. Sea slightly phosphorescent at night.

Jan. 26th, 43° 10′ S. 54° 17′ W.—Prion petrels, stormy petrels, like Wilson's, only more white on their breasts and wings; and a petrel, like a blue one, only with more white on its under-surface. During the afternoon a school of sperm whales came quite close to the ship disporting themselves. A piece of kelp was picked up, with barnacles and a lamellibranch attached to it.

Jan. 27th, 43° 33′ S. 55° 07′ W.—Prion petrels and an albatros were seen. Mr Bruce and Valette saw a great many examples of *Velella* between 6 and 8 P.M.

Jan. 28th, 45° 31′ S. 55° 21′ W.—A few small petrels, probably Wilson's, were the only animals seen to-day. Whilst the "Scotia" lay to for sounding, Johnnie Smith noticed some penguins.

Jan. 29th, 47° 47' S. 56° 08' W.—Mist all day. One petrel, probably a prion, and some penguins were seen.

Jan. 30th, 50° 03' S. 57° 58' W.—Six molliemauks, a skua, seven albatroses, and penguins were seen during the day. Brown secured a rich haul of copepods in his tow-net to-day.

Jan. 31st to 9th February, Port Stanley, Falkland Islands.—During our stay in Port Stanley traps were lowered, and some interesting specimens were secured. We all made an excursion to Cape Pembroke Lighthouse, and shot several specimens of birds, rock geese,[1] a young king-quawk,[2] and three or four different species of small birds.

Another excursion was made to the Tussoc Islands in Port William, and more birds secured; jackass penguins,[3] shags and the pink-breasted and pink-footed gull.[4] External parasites were found on the penguins.

Several turkey buzzards, a nelly, skuas, steamer-ducks, terns and numerous black-backed gulls were seen. A sea-lion[5] was shot on the lower Tussoc Island; skin and skeleton preserved; stones and some fragments of shells were found in its stomach. It measured 10 ft. 8 ins. in length and scaled over 1200 lbs.

The large trap which we lowered in Port William on 2nd December last was picked up; the netting was torn to a great extent, thus losing, no doubt, a valuable catch; only two crabs were found in it.

Several rock-cod and another species of fish were found in the trap, besides some three or four species of molluscs. Several specimens of *Clupea sagax,* a kind of herring, extraordinary shoals of which visited the Falkland Islands about this time, were also secured.

Feb. 10th, 53° 22' S. 56° 05' W.—Seven albatroses and some Wilson's petrels were the only birds seen to-day.

Feb. 11th, 55° 47' S. 54° 19' W.—Mist almost all day, except for a break about 5 P.M. Saw a blue petrel and some other petrels of two different species. One was about the same size as the blue petrel, with white on its under surface; the rest was dark, including the under surface of the wing. (Mr Bruce thinks this bird was a skua.) The other species was about the size of *Larus dominicanus,* or a little larger, and completely dark. Davidson saw a school of porpoises in the evening.

Feb. 12th, 57° 47' S. 51° 40' W.—A good many Wilson's petrels and blue petrels were following the ship all day. A few albatroses, molliemauks and the two new petrels (see yesterday's note) were also observed. Sea phosphorescent last night. A Cape pigeon was seen after tea.

---

[1] *Chloëphaga hybrida.*   [2] *Nycticorax obscurus.*
[3] *Spheniscus magellanicus.*   [4] *Larus glaucodes.*
[5] *Otaria jubata.*   Now in the Royal Scottish Museum, Edinburgh.

Zoological Log of Scottish National Antarctic Expedition.

[*Photo by Rowland Ward.*

66. Patagonian Sea Lion (*Otaria jubata*) in Royal Scottish Museum, from Tussock Island, Port William, Falkland Islands.
Weight, over 1200 lbs.

Feb. 13*th*, 59° 56′ S. 49° 30′ W.—Wilson's petrels, Cape pigeons and molliemauks very plentiful, as well as silver and blue petrels. A few sooty albatroses[1] and two skuas were seen, the latter eating the mutton we have on board. One of the men saw a large whale.

Feb. 14*th, Uruguay Cove, South Orkneys.*—Land sighted about 3 A.M. Anchored in Uruguay Cove about noon. Nellies, Cape pigeons, terns, snowy petrels, Wilson's petrels and a silver petrel were seen.

Feb. 15*th, Scotia Bay.*—Usual South Orkney birds.

Feb. 17*th, Scotia Bay.*—In the evening a party landed on the west shore and shot two Weddell seals, male and female. About fifty seals, all Weddells, were lying on the sandy beach.

Feb. 18*th, Scotia Bay.*—Mr Bruce, Valette, Kerr and I went to the west shore to get nellies and photographs of seals. Terns, a shag, Cape pigeons, nellies, skuas, snowy and Wilson's petrels and gulls were seen, besides gentoo penguins. A skua, two nellies and a penguin were secured with a view to preserving the brains. Some whales' bones were got on the west shore, including a zygomatic arch, a mandible and some vertebræ. About seventy seals (Weddells) were lying along the beach when we landed. One of them, a young one, had a wound at the nape of its neck, measuring about 7 inches in length and about 2 inches in width.

Feb. 19*th, Scotia Bay.*—Nellies, skuas, shags, penguins (adelia and ringed), terns, black-backed gulls, Wilson's petrels and Cape pigeons were seen during the day.

Feb. 21*st, Scotia Bay.*—Five cushion-stars, two other star-fish, four gasteropods, several pycnogons and three fish *(Notothenia)* were found in the trap to-day. One of the fish was given to a young *Lobodon*, captured on the North Beach a few days ago; the other fish were kept for his special benefit, but he does not appear to appreciate them. We have had him a week now, and he does not seem any tamer.

Feb. 22*nd.*—Left Scotia Bay at noon. Landed on Eillium Isle to slaughter penguins for food and specimens. Only ringed penguins were found, and we took both young and adult, also four adult paddies and one young. Saw a great many shags on the water and shot five. Two whales, probably finners, were seen off Saddle Island; for some time they were on the surface of the water and then disappeared. Nellies, skuas, Cape pigeons and Wilson's petrels were also seen very frequently.

Feb. 23*rd*, 61° 28′ S. 41° 55′ W.—A sooty albatros[2], a few snowy, blue and silver petrels, besides many Cape pigeons and Wilson's petrels were seen during the day. Mr Bruce and Fitchie saw a large albatros after tea.[3] Several finners were also observed during the day. Brown took a tow-netting at noon.

Feb. 24*th*, 62° 49′ S. 38° 12′ W.—A skua[4] (same as these in Laurie Island) was seen this evening, also a large albatros in the afternoon. A sooty albatros was hovering

---

[1] Probably *Phoebetria cornicoides*, Hutton's sooty albatros.
[2] This sooty albatros was *Phoebetria cornicoides*. Individuals of the species were sighted until 67° S. was reached.   [3] *Diomedea exulans.*   [4] The southern record for *Megalestris antarctica*.

I

round the ship in the morning. Cape pigeons and Wilson's petrels were constantly about the ship, with an occasional blue petrel. Several finners were also observed during the day. In the afternoon the otter surface trawl was let over the side and dragged for more than two hours; the catch consisted of one broken *Doliolum*. The young *Lobodon* which was captured on the North Beach disappeared this morning; it is supposed that it went overboard from the fo'c'sle head. A tow-netting was taken to-day.

Feb. 25th, 64° 29' S. 35° 29' W.—From six to eight terns[1] were seen in the afternoon. Cape pigeons, Wilson's petrels and blue petrels were constantly flying about the ship during the whole day. Sooty albatroses were also conspicuous; I saw about six of them at one time around the ship. A few snowy petrels and two or three antarctic petrels were seen during the afternoon and evening. Whilst sounding, a boat was lowered to enable me to shoot birds. I got both species of terns, five blue petrels[2] and one sooty albatros. Several finners were observed during the day.

Feb. 26th, 65° 59' S. 33° 06' W.—Entered the pack about 7 A.M. Few birds were seen to-day. Cape pigeons, antarctic petrels, snowy, Wilson's and blue petrels were flying about the ship at different periods of the day. Martin says he saw a nelly. A blue and two antarctic petrels were shot. Pirie shot a male sea-leopard in the afternoon. We all saw a great many specimens of *Euphausia* and two small fishes in the water whilst the ship was stopped for getting the sea-leopard on board. Brown saw many chains of what are possibly *Doliolum* in the evening. Some finners were also observed. Bright phosphorescence observed at intervals during the night.

Feb. 27th, 66° 26' S. 31° 25' W.—A few snowy petrels, one tern and two or three antarctic petrels were seen. Mr Bruce heard the cry of a penguin early in the morning. Three or four sea-leopards were seen during the day. One tunicate was caught on the sounding wire. Bright flashes of phosphorescence were caused by the propeller at intervals, giving a very beautiful light in the water.

Feb. 28th, 66° 21' S. 28° 30' W.—Many snowy petrels were seen during the day, and on two or three occasions in flocks of about fifty each; blue petrels were also frequently flying about, and a few antarctic and Wilson's petrels. Pirie shot a male Ross seal which had a very good skin, and whilst out shooting he saw a sooty albatros. I shot three snowy petrels and three blue petrels[3] in the evening. Pirie also saw penguin tracks on pieces of ice and some chains of what we think is *Doliolum*. Phosphorescence not so marked, and the flashes are less frequent than observed on the two previous nights. On dissection, the stomach of the Ross seal was found to contain cuttle-fish beaks, pieces of the mantle of a cuttle-fish and a mass of what appeared to be fish scales.

---

[1] *Sterna macrura*, the Arctic tern. All terns seen after this date belonged to this species.

[2] Both *Prion banski* and *Halobaena caerulea*. The latter species was not caught north of this latitude. On the following day *Prion banksi* alone was taken.

[3] The most southerly record for *Prion banksi*. South of this the blue petrels seen were *Halobaena caerulea*.

Feb. 29th, 68° 08' S. 27° 10' W.—Snowy and antarctic petrels, terns and two nellies were seen. Also many grampuses and a blast of another whale. The captain saw a penguin and heard others. A vertical net, eight feet in diameter, was lowered to a depth of 1000 fathoms. Contents were one fish, *Appendicularia*, a pteropod and three specimens of *Sagitta*, two jelly-fish, rather damaged, and a bright red crustacean, besides five other crustaceans, and what we suppose is *Salpa* or *Doliolum*.

Phosphorescence not marked to-night, only occasional flashes.

March 1st, 68° 43' S. 24° 15' W.—Snowy and antarctic petrels, a Wilson's petrel, two nellies, some terns, and also some grampuses were seen during the day.

March 2nd, 71° 04' S. 23° 10' W.—A nelly, antarctic, snowy and blue petrels, and black-headed terns were seen. Also grampuses.

March 3rd, 72° 18' S. 17° 59' W.—Nellies, very many antarctic and snowy petrels, and two or three terns were seen, as well as three emperor penguins, which we secured. Five snowy petrels, two antarctic petrels and one tern were shot. Many *Lobodons*, grampuses and whales were seen. Bird life has become much more abundant to-day, so that it was hardly a surprise when land was discovered to the south.

March 4th, 72° 22' S. 18° 13' W.—A great many antarctic petrels were flying about the ship especially in the evening. Snowy petrels were also plentiful. In addition, a Wilson's petrel and a tern were seen by Mr Bruce.

A great many seals were seen after dinner, swimming towards the north-west—they appeared to be *Lobodons*. Some whales were seen in the evening; their blast, according to the captain, differs from a finner's blast and resembles that of the northern bow-head whale. A few grampuses were sighted.

March 5th, 72° 31' S. 19° 00' W.—A big flock of terns was seen in the evening. Snowies were plentiful, and one nelly and some antarctic petrels were noticed. A good many seals (*Lobodon*) were amongst the ice-floes.

A vertical net was lowered down to a hundred fathoms before and after dinner. The contents of the two hauls were two species of pteropods, amphipods and other crustaceans, one ctenophore, a *Doliolum* or *Salpa*, chaetopods, and three or four long nemertean worms or tentacles of jelly-fish.[1] Grampuses and whales.

March 6th, 73° 30' S. 21° 28' W.—Terns, snowies and emperor penguins were abundant. The emperor penguins were all in the water, except one, which was found on a piece of ice and captured. A few adelias and about six nellies were also seen. A great many *Lobodons* were amongst the pack and swimming in the water.

March 7th, *Off Coats Land*, 74° 01' S. 22° 00' W.—A gale and snowstorm raging all day. Several *Lobodons* were seen in the morning and some emperors in the evening.

March 8th, *Off Coats Land*.—Gale and snowstorm not abated. One snowy and about ten emperors were seen in the evening. Three emperors were caught. Some seals were also seen.

[1] These have since been identified as the tentacles of a Siphonophore. See J. Rennie, *Proc. Roy. Phys. Soc., Edin.*, XVI., p. 25 (1904).

March 9th, Off Coats Land.—Wind gone down and altogether clearer to-day. A party went out this morning and captured fifteen emperors; two were brought alive to the ship. A nelly, an antarctic and a snowy petrel were seen. Brown shot a skua.[1] Macdougall shot a sea-leopard, but unfortunately it got away. Other seals were also seen, probably *Lobodons*.

March 10th, Off Coats Land.—Mr Bruce shot a female Weddell seal. *Lobodons* were seen. Two emperors were caught, and a few snowies and a skua seen. Large trap lowered down to bottom at 161 fathoms this evening.

March 11th, Off Coats Land.—The trap was hauled up this morning. Catch included three fish like the *Notothenia* caught in Scotia Bay, one isopod, three species of amphipods, and one bryozoan with sponges and a few worm-tubes attached to it. A nelly and a few snowies were seen. Many *Lobodons* and some Weddells.

March 12th, Off Coats Land.—The contents of the trap in 161 fathoms were one fish, many amphipods, a chaetopod and another worm, a crinoid, an alcyonarian and a sponge. There were more birds seen to-day, probably due to the ice breaking up and forming open "leads." Antarctic and snowy petrels, nellies, skuas and one emperor were seen, also *Lobodons*, a Weddell seal and a grampus.

March 13th, Off Coats Land.—Some snowy petrels and a few antarctic petrels. Many *Lobodons*, chiefly in the water, a Weddell seal and a sea-leopard were seen. Mr Bruce saw several bottle-noses and two grampuses. Kerr reports seeing two Ross seals swimming in the leads. A ctenophore and compound ascidian were also noticed. Mr Bruce saw tracks of an emperor this evening.

March 14th, 73° 11' S. 23° 53' W.—Very many antarctic and snowy petrels, also terns, flying about the ship to-day. Many emperors were seen this morning, also two nellies and two adelias. Shot about twenty antarctic petrels and fifteen snowy petrels.

A great many *Lobodons* and two grampuses were seen. The captain heard a finner blowing. Caught a *Euphausia* on a piece of pancake ice.

March 15th, 71° 50' S. 23° 30' W.—A great many antarctic and snowy petrels were flying about the ship during the whole day. One Cape pigeon and a good many terns were seen. The captain saw a finner.

A vertical net was lowered to 1000 fathoms and a fairly rich haul was made, including five or six species of fish,[2] several examples of *Doliolum*, four species of crustaceans, many specimens of *Sagitta*, several ctenophores, four species of medusoids and some broken pieces of a jelly-fish.

March 16th, 71° 28' S. 22° 32' W.—Antarctic and snowy petrels were constantly hovering round the ship, also numerous terns and blue petrels. A few adelias and a Cape pigeon were seen. A deep sea trawl was lowered down this morning—bottom

---

[1] *Megalestris maccormicki*.

[2] Including *Prymnothonus Hookeri*, Richardson (three specimens). The single existing specimen of this species previous to the *Scotia's* catch was taken by the *Erebus* and the *Terror*, 1843.

Zoological Log of Scottish National Antarctic Expedition.

[*Photo by W. S. Bruce.*

67. The "Scotia" beset off Coats Land, Antarctica. Shear Legs for baited trap set in 161 fathoms shown, also Flensing Board for Seal Skins.

[*Photo by W. S. Bruce.*

68. Weddell Seal (*Leptonychotes weddelli*), male, off Coats Land, Antarctica.

blue mud at 2338 fathoms—2830 fathoms of wire were paid out; the trawl came up twisted. It had evidently been fouled going down and had not reached bottom.

Many finners and grampuses were seen during the day. Flashes of phosphorescence observed at night like big blobs.

March 17th, 71° 22′ S. 18° 15′ W.—Antarctic and snowy petrels hovering round ship all day, though not in such quantities as yesterday. A few terns and Cape pigeons were seen. Also many grampuses and finners. Trawl lowered after breakfast, bottom at 2370 fathoms—3000 fathoms of wire rope were paid out, but it is extremely doubtful if bottom was reached. Dynomometer registered a strain of up to 2¾ tons. Trawl contained several specimens of (?) *Doliolum*, four species of coelenterates, mostly ctenophores or medusoids, and a cuttle-fish. Large blobs of phosphorescence were observed at night in the ship's wake about the size of this page.

March 18th, 71° 22′ S. 16° 34′ W.—Pirie and others saw a nelly early this morning. Snowy and antarctic petrels very abundant, especially the latter. A few Cape pigeons, terns and a silver petrel. Martin saw several antarctic penguins.

The trawl was let down in 1410 fathoms—2400 fathoms of wire rope paid out, dynomometer registering a strain of 2¾ tons. A rich haul was secured, including mud and several pebbles and small stones. At about 100 fathoms from the end the rope showed signs of having trailed along the bottom. The haul included :—about four species of fish,[1] two species of scaphopods, three species of gasteropods, some dead shells of lamellibranchs, a species of nudibranch, two of pycnogons, one cirriped, two other species of crustaceans, one species of brachiopod, seven or eight of polychaetes, three to six of ophiuroids, one crinoid, three echinoids, five species of asteroids, three to four of holothurians (one on a whale's ear-bone), three species of fixed colonial coelenterates, two species of medusoids, two of anemones, three of sponges and three foraminifers.

Pirie shot a male sea-leopard. Grampuses were sighted. Brown secured a rich haul of copepods in the tow-net.

March 19th, 71° 32′ S. 17° 15′ W.—Antarctic and snowy petrels very abundant, a nelly, terns and Cape pigeons also seen. During the afternoon several flocks of antarctic and snowy petrels and a nelly were seen settling down on the water, evidently feeding. The two emperor penguins which we have on board were fed to-night by Pirie, tinned herring being forced down their throats. The trawl was lowered down in 1221 fathoms, bottom blue mud, 2000 fathoms of wire rope being paid out; dynomometer registered a strain of 1½ tons. It turned out a failure, bottom not having been reached. Grampuses, finners and a sea-leopard were seen.

March 20th, 71° 17′ S. 18° 50′ W.—Antarctic and snowy petrels still abundant, following the ship all day, especially the former. One nelly and two silver petrels were seen. In the afternoon numerous blue petrels were hovering about the ship. Some Cape pigeons were observed. The emperor penguins were fed this evening. They

[1] Including *Bathydraco Scotiae* sp. nov.

swallow the tinned fish after it has been put into their mouths. Numerous grampuses and a few finners. Mr Bruce saw a fish something like a mackerel jump out of the water this afternoon. Sea very phosphorescent at night.

March 21st, 69° 33′ S. 15° 19′ W.—Antarctic and blue petrels fairly abundant. Also terns, two silver and a Wilson's petrel, many Cape pigeons and a number of new petrels[1] were seen, one of which Pirie shot, as well as one Cape pigeon, one antarctic, one silver and four blue petrels.

The trawl was lowered to 2620 fathoms, bottom blue mud ; 3600 fathoms were paid out, and the dynomometer registered up to five tons. The trawl came up with a great deal of mud and big stones and the following animals :—one fish, a worm off the wire about 600 fathoms from the end, arenaceous worm tubes, two species of asteroids, one species of ophiuroid, four species of holothurians, broken bits of echinoids, a medusoid, probably from the surface, two species of fixed stalked colonial coelenterates, two species of sponges, some species of foraminifers.

Some finners were seen. Brown secured some copepods in the tow-net this evening. Sea especially phosphorescent.

March 22nd, 68° 32′ S. 10° 52′ W.—Very few birds about to-day. A nelly, a few antarctic, blue and silver petrels, also a few terns and Cape pigeons. One or two finners sighted. A Cape pigeon, an antarctic petrel and a nelly were shot. Brown got copepods and very many radiolarians in his tow-net. Sea phosphorescent.

Mr Bruce saw a swimming bell and a jelly-fish. Two examples of *Doliolum* were caught on the sounding wire.

March 23rd, 68° 32′ S. 12° 49′ W.—Very many birds about to-day, blue petrels, antarctic petrels and Cape pigeons being most prominent, but also a few terns, two or three silver petrels, one snowy petrel and a dark nelly like the one shot yesterday.

The eight-feet vertical net was lowered to 800 fathoms for three hours. The catch included three fish, many examples of *Doliolum,* a cuttle-fish, two species of crustaceans, many specimens of *Sagitta,* several specimens of a species of polychaete, and a mangled medusoid. Many grampuses and finners.

March 24th, 68° 41′ S. 12° 36′ W.—Two nellies, some antarctic, silver and blue petrels, also Cape pigeons noticed to-day, but the weather was misty so that we did not see a great many birds. Finners were also observed. A *Doliolum* came up on the Pettersen-Nansen water-bottle. A good deal of phosphorescence in the sea.

March 25th, 68° 26′ S. 11° 11′ W.—A nelly, antarctic, blue and silver petrels and Cape pigeons were seen. Martin saw the new petrel, the same species which Pirie shot on the 21st inst. A four-feet vertical net, generally used as a tow-net, was lowered, and secured a rich haul of at least three species of copepods and many specimens of *Sagitta* and *Doliolum.* A few finners were seen. Sea very phosphorescent.

March 26th, 67° 36′ S. 12° 05′ W.—Not many birds about to-day ; a few blue, antarctic and new petrels, also Cape pigeons. The four-feet vertical net was towed at

---

[1] *Oestrelata brevirostris*—an addition to the avifauna of the Antarctic regions.

Zoological Log of Scottish National Antarctic Expedition.

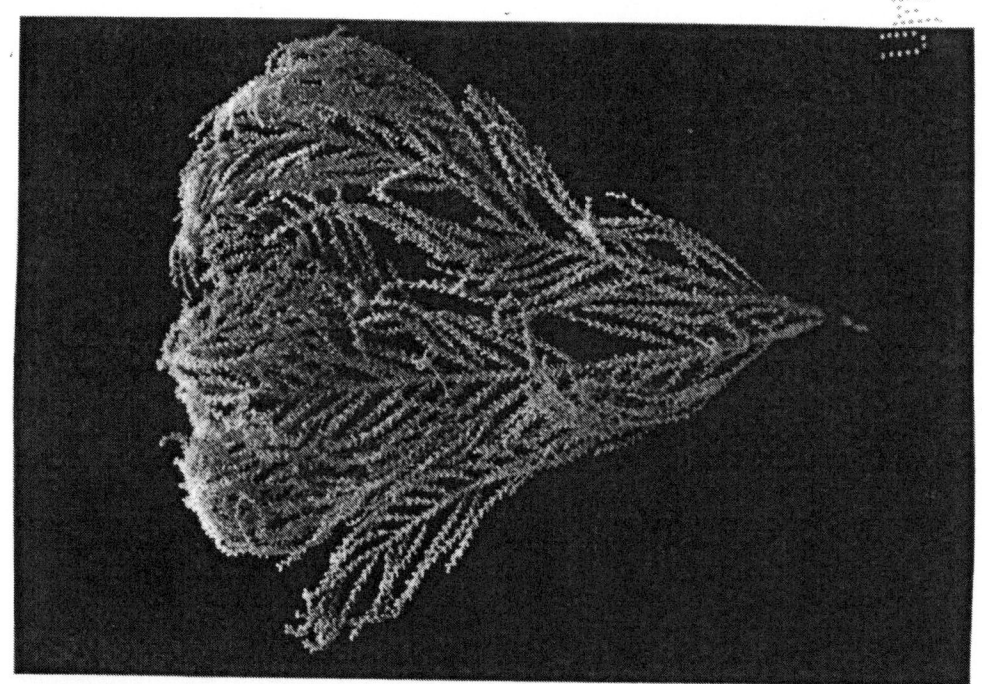

[Photo by W. S. Bruce.

71. An Alcyonarian (*Amphilaphis regularis*), taken in large quantities off Gough Island, South Atlantic, in 100 fathoms, and in smaller quantities at St Helena and Burdwood Bank. (⅔ natural size.)

[Photo by W. S. Bruce.

70. A New Species of Stalked Deep-Sea Crinoid or Feather-Star (*Ptilocrinus bruci*), taken from a depth of 2485 fathoms. Lat. 64° 48′ S., long. 44° 26′. (About ⅓ natural size.)

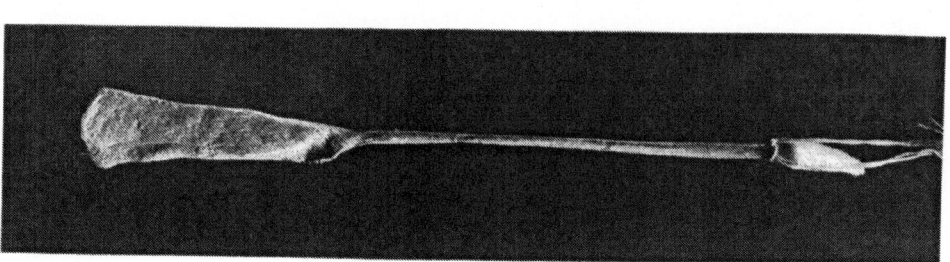

[Photo by W. S. Bruce.

69. A Stalked Deep-Sea Sponge. A New Genus and Species of the Family *Euplectellidæ*, taken from a depth of 2485 fathoms. Lat. 64° 44′ S., long. 44° 26′ W. (About ⅓ natural size.)

two fathoms below the surface. A rich haul was secured, including a great quantity of *Doliolum*, three or four species of amphipods, three or more species of copepods, many examples of *Sagitta*, two species of pteropods and a medusoid. The larger amphipods were associated with *Doliolum*, many being found in the atrium. The paddy which was brought alive from the South Orkneys died to day. The captive emperors are still alive. When weather permits we take them for a walk round the deck.

March 27th, 66° 57′ S. 11° 13′ W.—A nelly, a few sooty albatroses,[1] one big albatros,[2] some blue and the new petrels and Cape pigeons were seen during the day. Not many birds about—weather rather misty and overcast. One finner seen in the morning.

March 28th, 65° 58′ S. 11° 24′ W.—Several sooty albatroses, the new petrel, and a bird like the new petrel, only larger, some Cape pigeons and blue petrels, and two silver petrels were seen during the day. Not many birds altogether, but more than yesterday. Some grampuses and finners. The eight-feet vertical net was lowered to a depth of 50 fathoms for an hour and a quarter, and a rich haul of *Doliolum* was secured.

March 29th, 63° 54′ S. 10° 42′ W.—A silver petrel, blue petrels, and Cape pigeons, the new big petrel and sooty albatroses were seen during the day. Not many birds about as there was a strong gale blowing all day. Sea phosphorescent.

March 30th, 61° 25′ S. 12° 47′ W.—A few silver petrels, many blue petrels and Cape pigeons were flying about the ship. Shot four silver petrels and a black nelly; the latter bird was lost however. The captain saw a Cape hen and a drove of small penguins in the water; some small penguins were also seen on a small berg, probably black-throated, but too far off to distinguish. An albatros and some sooty albatroses about the ship. A considerable number of chains of *Doliolum* were seen and several were caught. The Cape hen is probably the new big petrel which has been seen on the 28th and 29th inst. The two captive emperors are getting quite used to tinned fish; the smaller one this morning opened its beak without compulsion, so we only had to put the food inside its mouth.

March 31st, 60° 37′ S. 12° 16′ W.—Sea very phosphorescent. More silver petrels seen to-day than at any other time since leaving the South Orkneys. Many Cape pigeons, and blue petrels, a nelly, a Cape hen (? petrel), a big albatros (almost all white) and sooty albatroses.

April 1st, 60° 33′ S. 12° 00′ W.—Many birds about all day long—several sooty albatroses, silver and blue petrels, as well as Cape pigeons, with an occasional nelly, were constantly about the ship. A white nelly was seen. Some ringed penguins were observed in the water about noon. A few Wilson's petrels were seen yesterday and to-day.

April 2nd, 58° 40′ S. 12° 23′ W.—A few nellies, some Cape pigeons, blue and silver petrels, sooty albatroses and Wilson's petrels. Birds not numerous, probably on account of bad weather.

[1] The most southern record for *Phoebetria cornicoides*.
[2] *Diomedea exulans*. The *Scotia's* most southerly record for the wandering albatros.

April 3rd, 56° 55′ S. 10° 00′ W.—Very many birds to-day, sooty albatroses, Cape pigeons and blue petrels being most conspicuous. Silver petrels not so numerous to-day. Specimens of the small new petrel[1] were seen several times before tea. About six nellies and some albatroses were also seen. Three sooty albatroses, a nelly and a large albatros were shot. Some penguins were sighted by Davidson and Pirie, too far off to distinguish the species. Wilson's petrels also seen. Many whales were disporting themselves nearly all day long, hunchbacks being the most conspicuous.

Sea phosphorescent at night.

April 4th, 55° 08′ S. 10° 00′ W.—Three new birds seen to-day—one, a sooty albatros[2] with a yellow line on its beak in place of the blue line on the beak of the ordinary sooty albatros; the second, a petrel about the same size as a blue petrel or perhaps larger, brown on its upper surface, white on its under surface, with a dark ring round its neck; third,[3] a petrel the same size and colour as a Wilson's petrel, with this difference that its abdomen and half the lower surface of the wing was white. Several Wilson's petrels, blue petrels, Cape pigeons and sooty albatroses were flying about the ship all day long.

Sea phosphorescent at night. Yesterday a four-feet vertical net was trailed along the surface; however nothing of zoological interest was caught.

April 5th, 55° 25′ S. 13° 10′ W.—Mr Bruce observed a new bird about the size of a Cape pigeon, more slender in build, general colour pale grey, darker on the upper surface of the wings and on the top of the head, white muzzle, dark eye, blackish beak, brownish ring round the neck, most of the under surface white. Another bird seen by Mr Bruce was about the size of a blue petrel, only much darker, brown rather than blue grey, a small white patch on its breast. Other birds seen same as yesterday.

Sea phosphorescent.

April 6th, 54° 33′ S. 11° 47′ W.—Nothing new noticed, except some floating kelp. Whales were seen. •

April 7th, 53° 58′ S. 10° 10′ W.—Three terns and several sooty albatroses were seen, both with the blue and yellow line on the beaks; a specimen of the latter was caught on a hook by Mr Bruce. Large albatroses and two kinds of Wilson's petrels also observed. One new bird was noticed to-day about the size of a Cape pigeon, possibly larger, colour same as a sooty albatros (probably same as Pirie shot about fourteen days ago and called the new petrel).[4]

The petrel with a ring round its neck and the grey-bodied petrel were also seen, the latter bird in large numbers. Brown saw a whale and the captain three or four grampuses. Sea very phosphorescent.

April 8th, 52° 33′ S. 9° 47′ W.—Blue-and yellow-billed sooty albatroses and *Diomedea melanophrys* were hovering about ship all day long. Fitchie observed a

---

[1] This was again *Oestrelata brevirostris.*

[2] *Phoebetria fuliginosa.* The other sooty albatros is *P. cornicoides.*   [3] *Cymodroma grallaria.*

[4] See note at March 21st.

Zoological Log of Scottish National Antarctic Expedition.

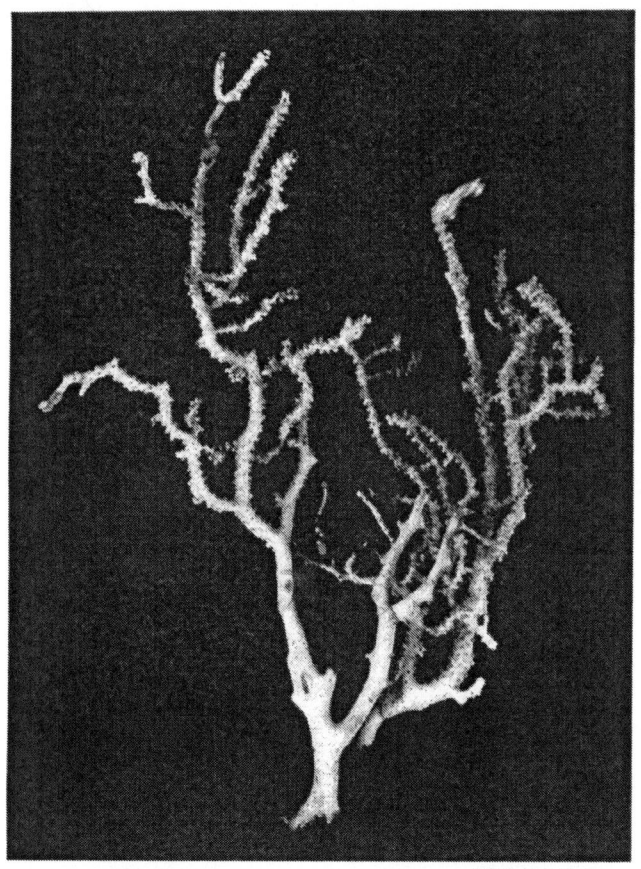

[*Photo by T. C. Day.*

72. An Alcyonarian (*Paramuricea robusta*) taken off Gough Island
in 100 fathoms, and off St Helena. (⅓ natural size.)

[*Photo by T. C. Day.*

73. A New Species of Alcyonarian (*Thourella brucei*) of
Gough Island, 100 fathoms. (⅔ natural size.)

[*Photo by T. C. Day.*

74. A Shallow Water Antarctic Buckie (*Neobuccinium
etoni*) taken in large quantities in Scotia and Jessie
Bays, South Orkneys. (Natural size.)

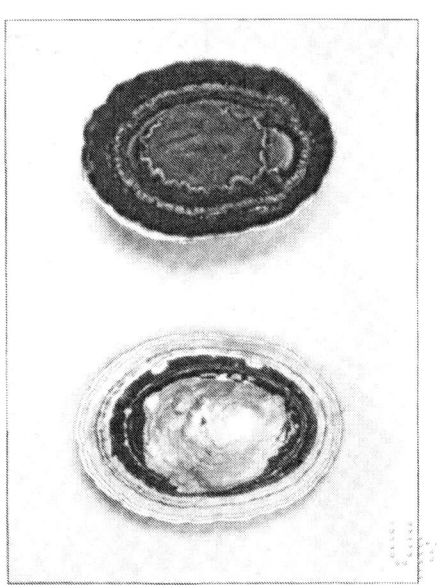

[*Photo by T. C. Day.*

75. A Shallow Water Antarctic Limpet (*Patella polaris*)
taken in large quantities in Scotia and Jessie
Bays, South Orkneys. (Natural size.)

couple of penguins, too far off to distinguish the species. White-bellied Wilson's petrels, the diving petrel, grey-bodied petrels, black-backed petrels,[1] terns and one Cape pigeon comprise the list of birds seen. Mr Bruce shot two yellow-billed sooties.

Sea very phosphorescent.

April 9th, 51° 07′ S. 9° 31′ W.—Blue- and yellow-billed albatroses and also *Diomedea melanophrys* about the ship continually; grey-bodied petrels, new petrels, two kinds of Wilson's petrels, one blue petrel, one Cape pigeon, terns, two species of penguins, one a jackass *(Spheniscus magellanicus)* and the other probably *Eudyptes chrysocome,* and the diving petrel *(Pelecanoides).* Mr Bruce saw a new albatros of the size and shape of *Diomedea melanophrys* and of the same colour except the back of its neck which was dark with a dark ring complete, or almost complete, round about it, and a black beak. Mr Bruce shot a blue- and also a yellow-billed albatros. The Monagasque trawl was lowered in 2103 fathoms with 3100 fathoms of wire-rope. On hauling it up some wire got twisted round the trawl and it came to the surface bottom up. Dynomometer registered a strain of 3½ to 4 tons. Some diatom ooze was got in the trawl and one star-fish, two ophiuroids, a sponge, a crustacean and an unrecognisable jelly-looking substance. Probably the bottom was rocky. Sea phosphorescent.

April 10th, 49° 25′ S. 9° 21′ W.—Sooty albatroses, both blue- and yellow-billed, large albatroses, grey-bodied petrels, and both kinds of Wilson's petrels were about the ship all day long—also one blue petrel and one Cape pigeon. A new petrel, about the size and shape of the grey-bodied petrel, white below except the throat which, with the whole of the dorsal surface of the bird, was light greyish-brown.[2] A new albatros was seen to-day, similar in size and shape to the one described yesterday and also similar in colouration, except that the whole of the head and throat were of the same greyish-brown colouration as the dorsal surface. The whole of the under surface of the wings was white except round the edges which were of the same greyish-brown: the top of the beak was yellow.

Sea phosphorescent to-night.

April 11th, 48° 53′ S. 9° 25′ W.—Several nellies, yellow- and blue-billed sooty albatroses, large albatroses, new albatros seen yesterday, two blue petrels, two Cape pigeons, jackass and macaroni penguins, grey-bodied petrels, new petrels and both kinds of Wilson's petrels. The emperors we have on board are getting very thin and appear to be very dejected.

Sea phosphorescent at night.

April 12th, 48° 00′ S. 9° 50′ W.—Blue- and yellow-billed albatroses, the new albatros (see description of the 10th inst.; we now call it the Burdwood Bank albatros), *Diomedea melanophrys,* a blue petrel, numerous grey-bodied petrels, black-backed petrels and both kinds of Wilson's petrels were about the ship. Mr Bruce caught a yellow-billed sooty albatros by means of a fishing line.

The deep-sea trawl was let down to the bottom (rocky) at 1332 fathoms: 2300 of

---

[1] *Oestrelata mollis.*   [2] *Priofinus cinereus.*

K

wire rope were paid out. The dynomometer registered a strain of a little over two tons. Very poor catch although most likely it reached bottom. The catch included four or five fish, three species of decapods, several examples of *Sagitta*, one medusoid and four different ctenophores.

April 13th, 48° 06′ S. 10° 05′ W.—One of the emperor penguins died to-day, and the other appears to be dying. Blue- and yellow-billed sooty albatroses, the Burdwood Bank albatros (see 1st Dec. 1903), nellies, Cape pigeons, white-bellied Wilson's petrels, one or two blue petrels, grey-bodied petrels and several petrels about size and shape of a silver petrel (see also the 10th inst.), of a uniform light-brownish-grey, except on the breast and abdomen, where the bird is white.[1] Monagasque trawl let down in 1742 fathoms, rocky bottom ; over 2900 fathoms of wire-rope were paid out, and the dynomometer registered a strain up to five tons. A fairly good catch was secured, including three species of fish, several crabs, crab ova and other crustaceans, one pycnogon, one small mollusc, one worm, one holothurian (deep purple colour), several umbellulids,[2] three species of asteroids and about half a hundredweight of small stones.

April 14th, 46° 35′ S. 10° 10′ W.—Blue- and yellow-billed albatroses, a few blue petrels, both kinds of Wilson's petrels, grey-bodied petrels and the light-brownish-grey petrels were seen during the day, also some petrels like the new petrel which Pirie shot, only they appeared to be larger. The second and last emperor penguin was found dead this morning; both of them were injected. Porpoises observed. Sea phosphorescent.

April 15th, 45° 54′ S. 10° 04′ W.—Sooty albatroses, Burdwood Bank albatroses, *Diomedea melanophrys*, blue petrels, black-backed petrels with the dark ring round the neck, both kinds of Wilson's petrels and the light-brownish-grey petrels were seen to-day.

April 16th, 45° 25′ S. 10° 19′ W.—Very many birds about to-day. Both kinds of sooty albatroses, Burdwood Bank albatroses, *Diomedea melanophrys*, and the new albatroses with the black beak described on the 9th inst., many grey-bodied petrels and their allies with white underneath (see also the 10th and 13th inst.), blue petrels, both kinds of Wilson's petrels, nellies, the dark-backed petrels with the ring round their necks, new petrels similar to the specimen Pirie shot, and a petrel like the latter, except that it appeared to be darker in colour and slightly larger, and much slimmer round the head. Phosphorescence observed both last night and to-night, though not so brilliant as a week ago.

April 17th, 44° 30′ S. 9° 43′ W.—Same kind of birds as seen yesterday, and fairly numerous. A silver petrel was hovering around the ship the greater part of the morning. Several attempts have been made to hook some of these new birds, but so far no success has attended us, though the birds, especially the Burdwood Bank albatros and the black-beaked one, have nibbled at the bait. Phosphorescent sea.

April 18th, 43° 21′ S. 8° 30′ W.—Both kinds of sooty albatroses, Burdwood Bank albatros, and its ally the black-beaked albatros, and other varieties of these two, nellies,

---

[1] *Priofinus cinereus.*   [2] The very rare *Umbellula durissima.*

Zoological Log of Scottish National Antarctic Expedition.

[Photo by W. S. Bruce.

76. Yellow-billed Sooty Albatross (*Phœbetia fuliginosa*) flying. Off Gough Island, South Atlantic.

[Photo by W. S. Bruce.

77. Southern Great Black-backed or Dominican Gull (*Larus dominicanus*) flying. South Orkneys.

two skuas, two Cape pigeons, many blue petrels, both kinds of Wilson's petrels, the grey-bodied petrel (see the 16th inst.) and black-backed petrels were seen during the day. A new bird was seen to-day by Mr Bruce about the size and shape of a Cape pigeon, the head, back, neck, tail and wings being of a dark brown colour, whilst the breast and abdomen were white ; also another bird of about half the size with a white mark on its cheeks. White, piebald and black porpoises were also seen.

April 19th, 42° 57′ S. 8° 13′ W.—Very many albatroses, a few Burdwood Bank and black-billed albatroses, three or four *Diomedea melanophrys*, two or three nellies, two skuas, a few Wilson's petrels, grey-bodied petrels and the light-brownish-grey petrels and a few blue petrels were seen.

April 20th, 41° 30′ S. 9° 55′ W.—Very many sooty albatroses, chiefly yellow-billed, a few black-billed and some young albatroses, a nelly and a skua, a few Wilson's petrels, very many light-brownish-grey petrels, black-backed petrels[2] and blue petrels were seen, also a tern which Walker caught. The four-feet vertical net was lowered and trailed along at a depth of about two to three fathoms ; one crustacean was caught. Sea very phosphorescent.

April 21st, Gough Island, 40° 20′ S. 9° 56′ W.—Too rough to land. Many birds were flying about the ship all day long. The following were spotted :—both kinds of sooty albatroses, particularly the yellow-billed, many wandering albatroses, *Diomedea melanophrys*,[1] many nellies and skuas, a great number of blue petrels, black-backed petrels,[2] grey-bodied petrels,[3] light-brownish-grey petrels,[4] both kinds of Wilson's petrels, especially the white-bellied ones,[5] and terns like the South Orkney species, one, however, with a brownish back.[6] Pirie and Karl caught a quantity of seaweed, on which were many amphipods of one species, an isopod and a stalked-eyed crustacean (schizopod) and several bryozoa. A large trap was lowered in the evening in about 70 fathoms, about a mile from shore. Sea very phosphorescent.

April 22nd, Gough Island.—A landing was effected this morning on Gough Island. Just before leaving, a black petrel[6] was seen. The following birds were secured :—four skuas,[7] several finches of two species,[8] four brown-backed terns,[9] two dead penguins,[10] one South Orkney tern,[11] a pair of petrels like blue petrels[12] (which Pirie heard croaking in a deep hole), four water-fowls[13] and an albatros.[14] A fish, several limpets, a chiton and two or three species of crustaceans were collected on the shore, and several millipedes, spiders, slaters, flies and a water-beetle were got ashore, the latter in a fresh water (stagnant) pool. A dead mouse[15] was found. Whilst we were away, the cooks caught six sooty albatroses, one of which spewed up a cuttle-fish. The bo'sun caught a

---

[1] A doubtful record for Gough Island : no specimens were secured : it may have been *Thalassogeron eximus.*   [2] *Oestrelata mollis.*   [3] The same as the following species (?)   [4] *Priofinus cinereus.*   [5] *Cymodroma grallaria.*   [6] *Majaqueus aequinoctialis.*   [7] *Melagestris antarctica.*   [8] *Nesospiza goughensis* sp. nov., and *N. jessiae* sp. nov.   [9] *Sterna vittata.*   [10] *Eudyptes chrysocome.*   [11] This record appears to be an error.   [12] *Puffinus assimilis.*   [13] *Porphyriornis comeri.*   [14] *Thalassogeron* sp. See Mr. W. Eagle Clarke's report on the birds.   [15] *Mus musculus*—evidently escaped from a ship on some previous occasion.

diving petrel.[1] Crested penguins[2] were seen on shore. A small trap was lowered in the morning and lifted in the afternoon—contents nil.

April 23rd, Gough Island.—The large trap, lowered on the 21st inst., was hauled up with all the bait gone and a big tear in it, so that only small animals were obtained, including some small crabs, a pycnogon, ophiuroids, pectens, a polychaete and other small invertebrates. After dinner, went out in dinghy and shot the following birds :—both kinds of Wilson's petrels,[3] black-backed petrels,[4] light-brownish-grey petrels,[5] a black petrel[6] (not the one seen yesterday however), brown and black nellies,[7] a whale bird,[8] *Diomedea melanophrys*[9] and *Diomedea exulans*. Yellow-billed sooties, terns, skuas and petrels,[10] like the pair Pirie caught yesterday, were seen.

The small trap was hauled up to-day, bait all gone and contents nil. Johnnie Smith caught a fish on the line.

The Monagasque trawl was lowered in 100 fathoms for half an hour, and a rich haul was secured. The following is a rough list :—two species of fish (one specimen only of the one species), about five species of lamellibranchs, nudibranchs, gasteropods, two species of crabs, a few other small crustaceans, a (?) gephyrean, a polychaete, three or four species of ophiuroids, an *Antedon*, innumerable " corals" and " corallines," two species of alcyonarians and two species of sponges.

Another trawl was made in 25 fathoms. A small catch was secured, but the ship rolled too much to sort the catch before preserving. Whilst out in the boat I shot a Wilson's petrel and a blue petrel,[11] but they were picked by skuas before we could get up to them. Penguins (*Eudyptes chrysocome*) were seen.

April 24th, 39° 58′ S. 8° 36′ W.—Many sooty albatroses (yellow-billed), *Diomedea melanophrys* and wandering albatroses, light-brownish-grey petrels, black-backed petrels, both kinds of Wilson's petrels and blue or whale petrels were seen. A number of pteropods and a blue copepod were caught on the surface. Sea phosphorescent.

April 25th, 40° 22′ S. 5° 45′ W.—Plenty of blue-billed sooty albatroses, in addition to the birds seen yesterday, were flying about the ship.

April 26th, 41° 15′ S. 2° 38′ W.—Many of the larger birds (albatroses) were seen to-day, though fewer of the smaller ones. Many blue- and yellow-billed albatroses, *Diomedea melanophrys* and *Diomedea exulans*, some light-brownish-grey petrels, both kinds of Wilson's petrels, black-backed petrels and blue petrels or whale birds.

April 27th, 40° 33′ S. 0° 07′ E.—Many albatroses, blue- and yellow-billed sooties, *Diomedea melanophrys* and *Diomedea exulans*, one skua, a few light-brownish-grey petrels, many black-backed petrels, a few Wilson's petrels of both kinds and a few blue petrels or whale birds were seen during the day. Shot two *Diomedea melanophrys*, a yellow-billed and a blue-billed sooty.

---

[1] *Pelecanoides urinatrix.*　　[2] *Eudyptes chrysocome.*　　[3] *Oceanites oceanicus* and *Cymodroma grallaria.*
[4] *Oestrelata mollis.*　　[5] *Priofinus cinereus.*　　[6] It appears, however, to be *Majaqueus aequinoctialis.*
[7] *Ossifraga gigantea.*　　[8] *Prion vittatus.*　　[9] See note 1 on last page.
[10] *Puffinus assimilis.*　　[11] The whale bird, *Prion vittatus.*

Zoological Log of Scottish National Antarctic Expedition.

[Photo by W. S. Bruce.

78. An Œstrellata in the " Roaring Forties."

[Photo by W. S. Bruce.

79. Cape Pigeon (*Daption capensis*) flying.   Off South Orkneys.

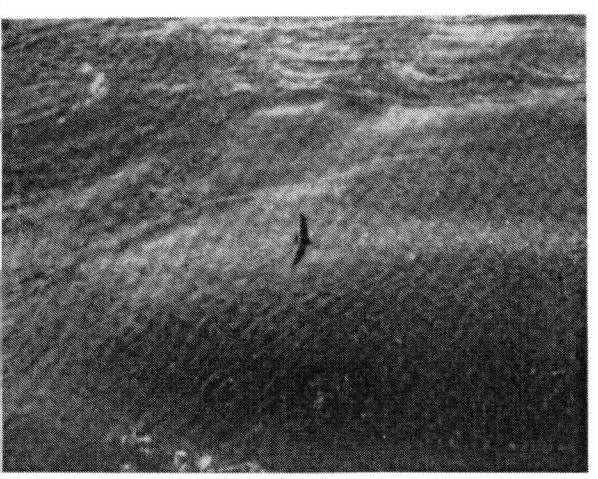

[Photo by W. S. Bruce.

80. Wilson's Storm Petrel (*Oceanites oceanicus*) flying.
Off South Orkneys.

[Photo by W. S. Bruce.

81. Blue-billed Sooty Albatross (*Phœbetria cornicoides*) flying.
About lat. 50° S., South Atlantic.

The four-feet vertical net was out—catch nil.

April 28th, 40° 08′ S. 1° 50′ E.—Very few birds seen to-day, misty weather. Sooty albatroses, *Diomedea melanophrys* and wandering albatroses, a few Wilson's petrels and light-brownish-grey petrels were seen.

The Monagasque trawl was lowered down in 2645 fathoms, bottom red clay, 3800 fathoms of wire rope paid out; dynomometer registered a strain up to $5\frac{1}{4}$ tons. When hauled up, a big hole was found in the cod-end, so that the catch was nil zoologically; a little mud (red clay) was found on the trawl itself.

April 29th, 39° 48′ S. 2° 33′ E.—More birds about to-day than yesterday; sooties were scarce to-day while *Diomedea melanophrys* and *Diomedea exulans* were plentiful, especially the latter. Very few "No. 9 Gough Island" petrels,[1] many "No. 14,"[2] and three or four black "No. 12" petrels,[3] one of which I shot, a few Wilson's petrels of both kinds and some blue petrels or whale birds. Shot three *Diomedea exulans*, one *Diomedea melanophrys*, and one black petrel, which is bigger than the one we saw on the 22nd inst. at Gough Island.

Trawled to-day with Monagasque trawl in 2645 fathoms in the same position as yesterday's attempt, bottom red clay; 4000 fathoms of wire were paid out, dynomometer registering a strain up to $4\frac{1}{2}$ tons. A small but representative catch was secured, of which the following is a rough list:—several small fishes of one species, one cephalopod, one lamellibranch and another broken mollusc, five species of crustaceans, one or two medusoids, three species of ophiuroids, three species of holothurians, one flat sea-urchin, one sipunculid, and some examples of *Sagitta* and ctenophores, probably from the surface.

One whale's ear-bone with some living animals attached to it was also found in the trawl.

April 30th, 39° 27′ S. 5° 50′ E.—A few sooty albatroses, some with a whitish ring round their necks, and evidently young, many *Diomedea exulans*, a few *Diomedea melanophrys*, "No. 9" and "No. 14 Gough Island" petrels (see April 29th), some black petrels like the one shot yesterday, several whale birds or blue petrels, and Wilson's petrels were seen. Some external parasites were found on the albatroses shot yesterday.

May 1st, 39° 25′ S. 10° 25′ E.—Sooties still few, many *Diomedea exulans* and *Diomedea melanophrys*, and also the other birds described in yesterday's log, were seen to-day. The black petrel with a white beak ("No. 12 Gough Island") was observed to-day. A school of porpoises or "black fish" was seen about noon.

May 2nd, 38° 06′ S. 14° 32′ E.—Same kind of birds seen to-day as yesterday, excepting "No. 9 Gough Island" petrel, which was not noticed.

May 3rd, 35° 37′ S. 15° 03′ E.—Very few birds seen to-day except a few "No 14 Gough Island" petrels, *Diomedea exulans*, *Diomedea melanophrys* and also a sooty albatros.

May 4th, 34° 58′ S. 17° 00′ E.—More birds seen to-day than yesterday. A few

---

[1] *Priofinus cinereus.*   [2] *Oestrelata mollis.*   [3] *Majaqueus aequinoctialis.*

" No. 12 " and " 14 Gough Island " petrels, and black petrels like the one shot on the 29th ult., some yellow-billed sooty albatroses, one blue-billed sooty, many *Diomedea exulans*, both young and adult, and a Wilson's petrel were seen. Sea very phosphorescent to-night ; more marked to-night on account of the moon not rising till later.

Some fish about the size of a porpoise were seen swimming in the water at night, their trail showing very plainly owing to the phosphorescence of the sea in their wake.

May 5th, Arrived at Cape Town.—Several birds were seen to-day. *Diomedea exulans*, yellow-billed and blue-billed sooties, *Diomedea melanophrys*, skuas, gannets, " No. 12 Gough Island " petrels, black petrels and Wilson's petrels. The captain and others heard sounds like penguins' cries, and Pirie and others saw something in the water which was either a penguin or a seal. Numerous porpoises were seen.

Sea very phosphorescent at night.

.   .   .   .

May 18th.—Left Cape Town last night, steaming slowly for Dassen Island, which we made soon after daybreak. A party went off in the boat to land, which, however, was impossible or too risky on account of a heavy surf beating on the shore. We could see numerous penguins on shore amongst the rocks and also on the water. Shags, gannets, black-backed gulls, Cape hens (*Majaqueus aequinoctialis*), also a grey gull with pink feet were seen.

The otter trawl was let down in the afternoon in 30 to 40 fathoms, dynomometer registering two to three tons ; 100 fathoms of wire-rope were paid out. The trawl was down for half-an-hour and a fairly good catch was secured, including eleven dog-fish and several other species of fish, three species of cuttle-fish, a nudibranch, two species of crabs, one species of crayfish, two species of pycnogons, one species of chaetopod, two species of asteroids, one species of alcyonarian, a sponge and some bryozoa.

In the evening we anchored in Houtjes Bay, Saldanha Bay, and dropped a vertical net over the stern in five fathoms. On hauling it up we found a coffer-fish, three buckies and a small crab. The live monkey, which we took from Cape Town Museum yesterday afternoon, had to be killed this morning as he bit one of the staff very badly on the leg.

May 19th, Houtjes Bay, Saldanha Bay.—In the morning Brown, Pirie, Johnnie Smith and I went along the shore towards the other end of the bay, where the ship was to anchor for the night. The shore was covered with shells of various kinds, lamellibranch, gasteropods and cuttle-fish. We struck inland for some time, where Pirie shot some small birds (about six), and we collected some millipedes, some beetles and two or three lizards. Along the shore a (?) sanderling, a grey-backed gull [1] similar to the South Orkney gull and having the red ring round the eye, and a black bird with a bright crimson bill and darker crimson legs were shot.

A rich haul was secured by means of the vertical net, consisting of many fishes, cuttle-fish, buckies, crabs, etc.

A trawl (double-headed deep-sea) was let down in eight fathoms and brought up

---

[1] Identical with the southern species *Larus dominicanus.*

Zoological Log of Scottish National Antarctic Expedition.

[*Photo by W. S. Bruce.*]

83. Bush completely covered with Nests, probably Shags', on an island in Saldanha Bay, South Africa.

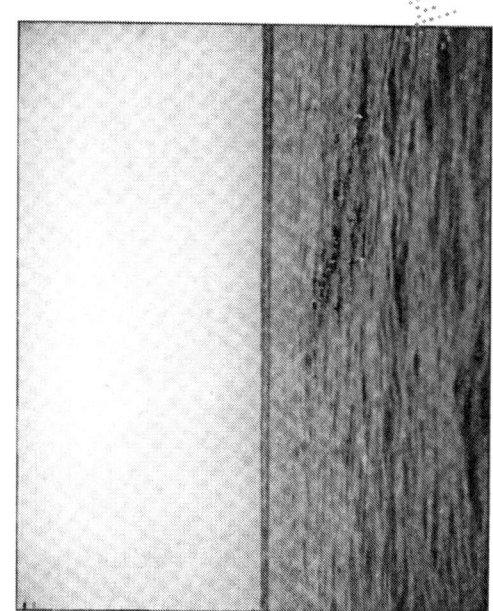

[*Photo by W. S. Bruce.*]

85. Jackass Penguins (*Spheniscus demersus*) off Dassen Island, South Africa.

[*Photo by W. S. Bruce.*]

82. His Excellency Col. H. C. Galway, Governor of St Helena, riding on a Tortoise introduced into St Helena about 100 years ago.

[*Photo by W. S. Bruce.*]

84. Jackass Penguins (*Spheniscus magellanicus*) on Tussock Island, Port William, Falkland Islands.

a large quantity of sea-urchins, a few brittle stars, two small fishes, a small cephalopod, a small chaetopod and a considerable quantity of broken shells.

About 100 young sharks and several gurnards were caught by means of the line.

A considerable quantity of marine life was collected on the rocks ashore.

May 20th, Off Salamander Point, Saldanha Bay.—A number of small isopods were caught in the trap. A party went in the whale boat to Mieuw Island to collect. Whilst there we came across what looked like miniature hay-stacks, composed of dry sticks from 4 to 5 ft. high and as much across. On pulling these down we found some eggs which appeared to be like shags, and apparently these stacks are built in successive layers year by year. Caterpillars very abundant on the island. A good deal of shore-collecting was done.

Afterwards we set a trammel net at the mouth of Reit's Bay. On hauling it up we found many sharks of a different species to the ones caught yesterday, and a small pipe-fish and another fish.

A landing was also made on the south side of Reit's Bay where a good collection of beetles was made and a live tortoise was secured.

Saw a great many ibises [1] and shags [2] but failed to get within range of them. Numerous gulls, black and grey-backed, two kinds of (?) sanderlings and a number of small land birds were seen, as well as two deer.

May 21st, Saldanha Bay.—Went with the boat early this morning to pick up the trammel net : a good catch of sharks and other animals was secured.

Weighed anchor a little before noon and stopped at Marcus Island, where we tried to land but found it too risky owing to the heavy surf. Shot two shags off the island. Trawled in 25 fathoms at the entrance of Saldanha Bay with an otter trawl and caught the following :—about eight species of fish, two species of crustaceans, a large number of big crayfish, and a whole host of other animals, which we had no time to sort. Quite a record catch.

Saw numerous shags, gannets and (?) pipers, and a flock of ibises in the morning.

May 22nd, 31° 38′ S. 15° 15′ E.—Many Cape hens, skuas, and *Diomedea exulans* were seen, also a Cape pigeon and a Wilson's petrel.

May 23rd, 30° 05′ S. 12° 35′ E.—Saw two petrels, too far off to distinguish the species. The captain saw three gannets.

May 24th, 28° 19′ S. 9° 56′ E.—Two albatroses, *Majaqueus aequinoctialis* and a " No. 14 Gough Island " petrel [3] were the only birds seen to-day.

May 25th, 26° 12′ S. 7° 05′ E.—More birds seen to-day, many " No. 14 Gough Island " petrels, a Wilson's petrel, a Cape pigeon, many *Majaqueus aequinoctialis* and albatroses (*Diomedea exulans*).

May 26th, 24° 14′ S. 4° 32′ E.—Many " No. 14 Gough Island " petrels, one Cape pigeon, a white-bellied storm petrel (*Majaqueus aequinoctialis*) and several *Diomedea exulans* were seen during the day.

[1] *Ibis aethiopica.*　　　[2] *Phalacrocorax capensis.*　　　[3] *Oestrelata mollis.*

May 27th, 22° 23′ S. 1° 42′ E.—Martin saw an albatros, a *Majaqueus aequinoctialis* or Cape hen, and a small bluish bird, evidently a whale bird from his description of the beast.

May 28th, 19′ 45′ S. 0° 35′ W.—Only one bird seen to-day, a "No 14 Gough Island" petrel. Mr Bruce took a photograph of a bottle-nose quite close to the ship.

May 29th, 17° 25′ S. 2° 34′ W.—Three flying-fish were observed by three of the crew. Haimes saw a whale's "spout."

May 30th to *June 2nd, St Helena.*—During our stay two small traps and the large trap were set two or three times and some material collected, mostly out of the big trap, which we left behind, since we could not find it on our departure; it had probably dropped off a ledge of rock into deep water. Several fish were caught by means of a line and a trammel net. Left St James Bay at 2 P.M. on June 2nd, and trawled about 1 mile or 1½ miles off the shore to the west in about 50 fathoms. The trawl fouled the first time and we got a very small catch; one fish, two small crabs, a sea-urchin, two or three polychaetes and some (?) compound ascidians. On putting out the trawl a second time, it got foul of the propeller and it took the men till nearly 6 P.M. to get it clear; they ultimately had to cut the trawl near the cod-end.

On June 1st I shot three different species of birds from the dinghy.

June 3rd, 14° 31′ S. 7° 05′ W.—No beasts seen to-day.

June 4th, 12° 40′ S. 9° 06′ W.—A flying-fish came on board last night; no other animals observed.

June 5th, 10° 46′ S. 11° 12′ W.—A gannet, a finner (?) and some flying-fish were seen.

June 6th, 8° 51′ S. 13° 20′ W.—Some gannets and flying-fish were seen.

June 7th, Ascension.—Several gannets and tailor birds seen flying and diving about the ship; three young gannets were caught.

In the afternoon a party of us went to Wide-awake Valley. There were no live birds at the place, though plenty of dead terns (*Sterna fuliginosa*) were scattered over the valley. Mr Bruce got a present of twelve terns' eggs from Mr Chalmers of the Cable Company.

Rankin and others caught some fish.

June 8th, Ascension.—A party went to the top of Green Mountain. Near the summit we saw two kinds of rats, two rabbits, a partridge, a white bird like the one obtained at St Helena, and "miner" birds—black with large white round marks on the wings—and a few small birds. On the way Mr Bruce caught a land crab, which does not appear to be a common animal on the island. Shore collecting did not result in much, owing to the heavy surf.

Some fish were caught in the small trap lowered in 10 fathoms, as well as in the large trap in 18 fathoms. Visited the turtle ponds (*Chelone mydas*) in the morning and got a small turtle which we found dead.

Gannets and tailor birds were seen from the ship during the day.

Zoological Log of Scottish National Antarctic Expedition.

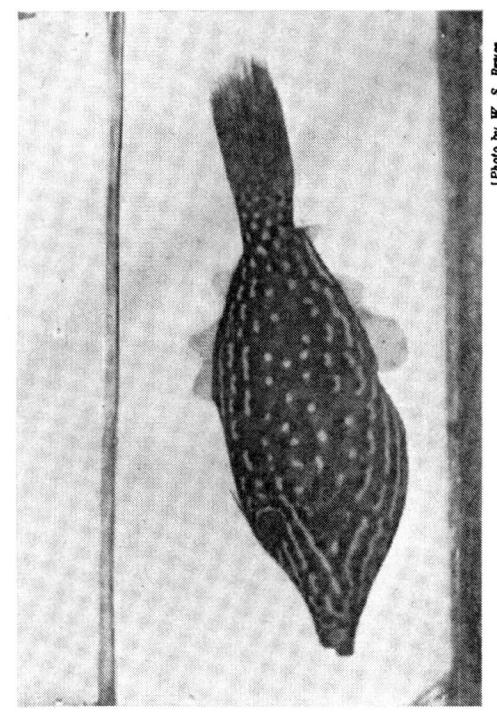

87. A Living Monocanthus. (⅓ natural size.)

[Photo by W. S. Bruce.

89. D. W. Wilton Shooting Birds in Mid-Atlantic.

[Photo by W. S. Bruce.

86. Two Living Chelmons and a Living Baby Turtle. (⅓ natural size.)

[Photo by W. S. Bruce.

88. J. H. H. Pirie Catching Velellas in Mid-Atlantic.

[Photo by W. S. Bruce.

June 9th, Ascension.—Same kinds of sea birds seen as yesterday. About a dozen species of fish were caught during the day; four large sharks besides other fish were in the trammel net which was badly torn by the former. A trumpet-fish was caught in the large trap and some others were found in the small traps. Several albacores[1] or a kind of tunny were caught by means of a line; the largest one weighed 105 lbs. One was used for food, another was sent ashore to Captain M'Alpine and two were preserved. Some other fish were caught on the line, but many hooks were carried away by the large tunnies. With the permission of Captain M'Alpine we secured two baby turtles from the turtle ponds and kept them alive on board in a tank.

June 10th, 7° 36′ S. 14° 33′ W.—Weighed anchor early in the morning and trawled in 40 fathoms off Pyramid Point before breakfast. Secured a very rich haul—about 130 fish altogether, of which about 100 were flat-fish. Whilst the trawl was out I went away in the dinghy and shot about a dozen birds in all, comprising three species, as far as I can make out, gannets, tailor birds and small black birds like the one shot at St Helena.

I landed on a rock near the shore and found gannets and the small birds busy in bringing up their young. They did not seem to have any nests, but simply laid their eggs on the bare rock. Some gannets had fresh laid eggs and others had chicks, some of which were big birds almost ready for flight. I did not see any of the black bird's eggs, though I secured some young ones which were not able to fly. There were a great many lice on the birds.

Porpoises, a Portuguese man-o'-war, wide-awakes and two or three white-bellied Wilson's petrels[2] were seen during the day.

June 11th, 4° 47′ S. 15° 47′ W.—*Physalia,* flying-fish, a gannet and a few white-bellied stormy petrels were seen during the day.

June 12th, 2° 46′ S. 17° 24′ W.—A school of porpoises were playing about the bows of the ship after breakfast; however, as soon as a harpoon was brought, they all vanished. Saw an albacore jump about four feet out of the water. A large Portuguese man-o'-war, two wide-awakes, flying-fish and a Wilson's stormy petrel were seen: the latter bird was too far off to distinguish the species. Sea very phosphorescent since leaving Ascension.

June 13th, 0° 15′ S. 18° 32′ W.—The captain saw two Wilson's petrels, probably the white-bellied ones, and also a flying-fish.

June 14th, 2° 09′ N. 19° 26′ W.—Numerous flying-fish were seen during the day. One jumped on board early this morning.

June 15th, 3° 50′ N. 19° 58′ W.—Flying-fish, porpoises and a shark were seen. Sea very phosphorescent.

June 16th, 6° 02′ N. 20° 33′ W.—The steward caught a shark, which we preserved. We failed to catch the two pilot-fish, which were striped like a zebra. Several porpoises, flying-fish and two or three stormy petrels, probably Wilson's, but too far off to distinguish.

[1] *Thynns albicora.* [2] Probably *Cymodroma grallaria.*

L

June 17th, 7° 25′ N. 21° 39′ W.—A bird, like a black-backed gull, black on the upper surface and white below, was seen before breakfast; also flying-fish. A shark was harpooned but got clear. Porpoises seen during the day.

June 18th, 9° 46′ N. 21° 34′ W.—Saw two small birds, too far off to distinguish the species, but probably Wilson's stormy petrels. Flying-fish and *Physalia* were conspicuous. Porpoises seen at night when the sea was very phosphorescent.

June 19th, 11° 32′ N. 20° 30′ W.—Wilson's petrels were seen this morning by Davidson, and an unknown bird about the size of a pigeon was seen flying about half a mile to starboard. Very many flying-fish were sporting about the ship all day long; five specimens of *Physalia* were caught.

June 20th, 13° 07′ N. 21° 47′ W.—Three or four stormy petrels, flying-fish and a shark were seen. One small fish was caught. Sea still very phosphorescent at night.

June 21st, 14° 27′ N. 23° 30′ W.—Davidson saw a bird, in size somewhat smaller than a booby, tail long and narrow like a bo'sun or frigate bird, under surface greyish white, upper dark colour. Martin saw two or three gannets. *Physalia* and flying-fish were seen frequently. At noon the island of St Jago, Cape Verde Islands, was sighted.

June 22nd, 15° 25′ N. 25° 20′ W.—Davidson saw about a dozen birds answering to yesterday's description. The captain and I saw three or four birds just before breakfast, of a whitish colour, with narrow wings tipped with black and a very long pointed tail—evidently frigate birds. Mr Bruce observed a bird about the size of a common gull, dark on the upper surface, white below. *Physalia* and flying-fish common.

June 23rd, 16° 55′ N. 26° 22′ W.—Same kind of birds seen as on the 21st inst. This bird is of a brownish black plumage except the breast, the abdomen and the middle part of the under surface of the wings, which are all white. *Physalia*, flying-fish and many bonitos were seen during the day.

June 24th, 18° 43′ N. 27° 46′ W.—Mr Bruce saw a bird of the same kind as seen yesterday.

June 25th, 20° 19′ N. 29° 10′ W.—Flying-fish were the only animals seen to-day.

June 26th, 22° 44′ N. 30° 35′ W.—A bird like a large stormy petrel, chiefly white on the under surface was seen by Mr Bruce. Flying-fish also observed.

June 27th, 25° 02′ N. 31° 51′ W.—Only flying-fish seen to-day.

June 28th, 27° 23′ N. 33° 06′ W.—Some cetaceans were seen to-day, greatly resembling "black-fish." Crabs, shrimps, hydrozoa, a gasteropod and a chaetopod were collected on some floating gulf-weed which was caught by means of a net.

June 29th, 29° 54′ N. 34° 10′ W.—Flying-fish were seen. A large quantity of gulf-weed passed the ship continuously in small or large floats and sometimes as many as four men were on the look-out to catch it. A good quantity was caught and a number of animals were found on it: fish, molluscs, a large number of crabs (about four species), other crustaceans, bryozoa, hydrozoa, etc.

Zoological Log of Scottish National Antarctic Expedition.

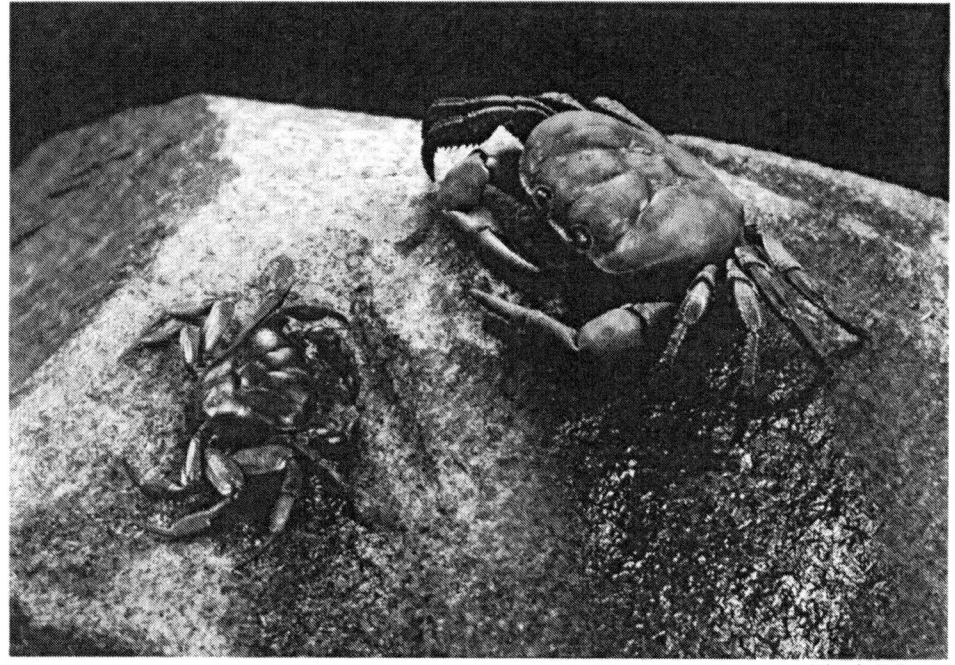

[Photo by T. C. Day.

90. Land Crabs (*Telphusa*) at an altitude exceeding 2000 feet on Green Mountain, Ascension.   (⅓ natural size.)

[Photo by T. C. Day.

91. A Cape of Good Hope Tortoise (*Testudo ungulata*, Schweigg) captured in Saldanha Bay, South Africa.
(⅓ natural size.)

June 30th, 32° 11′ N. 34° 10′ W.—Numerous flying-fish. Gulf-weed still continues to float past the ship; a great deal of it is caught and examined. Fish, nudibranchs, crabs, amphipods and shrimps, gasteropods, bryozoa, chaetopods, hydrozoa, etc., were found on the weed.

July 1st, 33° 53′ N. 32° 27′ W.—A few flying-fish were seen. Gulf-weed floating past the ship very frequently; many animals similar to those found yesterday were collected from it. Charlie caught three or four medusoids[1] and saw a turtle in the evening. These medusoids were phosphorescent at night.

July 2nd, 36° 05′ N. 30° 50′ W.—The captain and others saw two stormy petrels; species unknown. Davidson noted a grey tern.

Some gulf-weed floated past the ship to-day—a very small quantity of it, and none was caught.

July 3rd, 37° 41′ N. 29° 25′ W.—Several small stormy petrels, possibly Wilson's, another large petrel and a black-backed gull, possibly *Larus marinus*, were noted. A turtle floated past the ship. Pirie, MacDougall and Charlie caught several medusoids.[2] Amphipods were found living epizoically on them.

July 4th, 37° 56′ N. 29° 11′ W.—Shot nine Wilson's petrels and five large petrels. Saw the same gull that we noticed yesterday. Trawled in the afternoon on the *Princesse Alice* Bank[3] in 350 fathoms. The nature of the bottom is evidently very rocky, as the dynomometer showed considerable jerkiness, especially while the trawl was being hauled up, when we had frequently to delay hauling in order to ease the strain. Very poor catch indeed: about four pieces of sponge like *Hyalonema*, a few pieces of coral and a medusoid, the latter evidently from the surface.

A school of very white porpoises was seen. A few jelly-fish and swimming-bells were noticed passing the ship.

July 5th and *6th, Fayal, Azores.*—Saw a school of porpoises before entering the harbour. Visited the fish market, where Mr Bruce bought a number of different species for specimens. One fish was caught in the small trap.

July 7th, 39° 15′ N. 26° 55′ W.—Wilson's petrels were following in the wake of the ship all day. Several terns were seen in the afternoon. In the evening some large petrels, a school of porpoises and a large number of jelly-fish were noted.

July 8th, 40° 19′ N. 24° 47′ W.—A few Wilson's petrels and a large petrel, the same as yesterday, were seen, also a few porpoises.

July 9th, 41° 18′ N. 22° 25′ W.—A few Wilson's petrels and a large petrel, something like the ones shot on the *Princesse Alice* Bank, were the only animals seen.

July 10th, 42° 44′ N. 19° 30′ W.—A few Wilson's petrels and the large petrel, like the ones obtained on the *Princesse Alice* Bank, also some porpoises.

---

[1] *Aurelia solida.*   [2] *Pelagia perla.*
[3] The *Princesse Alice* Bank, discovered by the Prince of Monaco, extends from 36° 40′ N. to 38° 00′ N. and from 29° 07′ W. to 29° 25′ W., and has a depth of under 500 metres (273 fathoms).

July 11*th*, 44° 11′ N. 16° 05′ W.—A few Wilson's petrels about. A shark was seen this morning. Very many porpoises.

July 12*th*, 45° 56′ N. 12° 53′ W.—Very many porpoises and some Wilson's petrels.

July 13*th*, 48° 23′ N. 10° 22′ W.—A considerable number of porpoises and a few Wilson's petrels.

July 14*th*, 51° 13′ N. 7° 20′ W.—A few small petrels, probably *Procellaria pelagica*, as these breed on the Scilly Isles, but it is impossible however to distinguish this species from Wilson's petrel on the wing. The same remark applies to the last day or two. Mr Bruce saw two gannets (*Sula bassana*). Some herring gulls were also seen, and a bird resembling a common guillemot.

July 15*th*, 1904.—Arrived at *Kingstown, Ireland.*

Zoological Log of Scottish National Antarctic Expedition.

[Photo by W. S. Bruce.

92. Omond House, Scotia Bay, South Orkneys.

[Photo by L. H. Valette.

93. A Giant Cuttle Fish (Onychotenthis). Captured in Jessie Bay, South Orkneys. (Length about 6 feet).

Zoological Log of the Summer Station

"OMOND HOUSE," SCOTIA BAY, SOUTH ORKNEYS [1]

J. H. HARVEY PIRIE, B.Sc., M.D., Ch.B.,
Recorder

Nov. 27th, 1903.—Birds observed : skuas and terns fairly numerous, black-throated and ringed penguins, shags, a few nellies, black-backed gulls, snowy petrels and a pair of Wilson's petrels in the evening.

Nov. 28th.—Birds observed : skuas, terns, adelia and ringed penguins, shags, nellies, gulls, one of which in immature plumage was shot, snowy petrels and Wilson's petrels.

Nov. 29th.—Birds observed ; skuas—always numerous around the house after dead birds—terns, adelia and ringed penguins, shags, nellies, gulls in mature and immature plumage, a second of the latter kind being shot to-day. Snowy petrels numerous about the cliffs on the west side of Uruguay Cove.

Cape pigeons seen there also for first time for several days. A pair of Wilson's petrels over Jessie Bay.

One Weddell seal on the ice in Uruguay Cove. We dug through the frozen surface of a small pool which has formed on the northern part of The Beach and got about a foot of water ; amongst the stones at the bottom we found abundant collembolids,[2] in a very lively condition. These insects may be found under almost any stone.

Nov. 30th.—Birds seen : skuas, gulls, terns, adelia and ringed penguins, shags, nellies, paddies, snowy petrels and Cape pigeons. At Point Davis gulls' and terns' nests ; one gull's nest with three eggs, one with two which we lifted, and several with one (probably first one already taken).

Dec. 1st.—Got embryos of gentoo penguins, 10 to 18 days. A few gentoos are bold enough to peck at one in the rookery now, but most will still run from their nests ; but it is not so with the adelias, who all attack fiercely if one goes amongst them.

Gull's nest on beach at Point Martin. One egg had been taken from there about

---

[1] From November 27th, 1903, to February 14th, 1904, the *Scotia* was absent at Buenos Aires and the Falkland Islands coaling and refitting.

[2] *Isotoma Brucei* and *Cryptopygus crassus.* Both these new species occur in abundance at the South Orkneys.

ten days ago, so probably this would have been a nest of three eggs. Another nest with one egg was found on the top of the nearer of the two rocky islets close by here in Scotia Bay. I marked the eggs.

Took a tow-netting in Uruguay Cove and lifted the trap which was down in 9 fathoms; only amphipods in it, but these very abundant; they had cleaned a skeleton[1] in two days. Tried the otter trawl in 6 to 8 fathoms, but caught nothing.

Thirty to forty Weddell seals between here and the "Half-Moon" rookery, on the beach and on small floe-pieces. Observed one with a large festering sore on one hind flipper; area denuded of skin about 8 by 4 inches. Birds seen: adelia, gentoo and ringed penguins, shags, skuas, paddies, nellies, gulls, snowy petrels, terns and a few Cape pigeons.

Dec. 2nd.—Shifted trap into Scotia Bay. Two skuas' eggs were got to-day, both in one nest, and numerous ringed penguins' eggs. Also brought back marked gentoo eggs for embryos, 12 to 19 days, and three adelia eggs, the only marked ones we could find.

·On the cliffs on the west side of The Beach I got three Cape pigeons' eggs and two snowy petrels'. All had single eggs. The Cape pigeons, when approached, eject a nasty-smelling reddish fluid at one to a distance of as much as 8 feet, or usually 4 to 6 feet. They will not move off their nests, but allow themselves to be caught. Their nests consist merely of a few angular fragments of stone on a ledge or shelf of the rock. Eggs pure white and very large for the size of the bird.

The snowy petrels' nests are even rougher, with a very few stones, and are in a hole, crack or crevice of the rock, not lying exposed on a shelf. The bird, when approached, has a similar disagreeable habit to the Cape pigeon, but it is not quite so bad. It does not fly off its nest but retreats further back into the hole or crevice, and from there pours forth its offensive fluid, uttering all the time a series of shrill, harsh, discordant cries. There are also several dozen Wilson's petrels up in these cliffs and one was caught on its nest, which, like those of the snowy petrels, was in a very small crevice under a rock. The bird readily allowed itself to be caught. It brought up a little reddish fluid which came through the nostrils as well as out of the mouth, a fact which was observed with the snowy petrel also. No eggs were got. In addition to these birds, numerous gulls, nellies, shags, terns and paddies were seen. Weddell seals abundant along the west side of the bay.

Dec. 3rd.—At the ringed penguin rookeries. Most of the birds lay two eggs. Their rookeries are the dirtiest of the lot, which is saying a good deal. The birds are very fierce and bite viciously at one's legs. Their cries are also rather more shrill and harsh than those of other penguins.

Got a clutch of two terns' eggs. Saw one paddy's nest on a ledge under an overhanging rock, composed of small stones and tail feathers of penguins; no eggs.

Temperature under three penguins sitting on eggs 102°·7, 101°·0, 101°·4. Got

[1] The traps were generally baited with carcases of penguins or other birds.

three more Cape pigeons' eggs.   There were six birds sitting on nests on that particular ledge but only three have laid.   The eggs when blown proved to be all quite fresh, but those of the snowy petrel had been sat upon several days.

Got four more skuas' eggs (two clutches of two).   Their nests are on moss-covered rocks about a height of 200 feet, where they fashion hollows, smoothed off with loose pieces of moss.   Birds sit very close, one on the nest, the other close by.   When approached, they scream defiance and have to be forcibly ejected from the nest; not altogether a safe proceeding since the other bird wheels round close to one's head in a threatening fashion, though one never actually touched us.

Gull's nest on nearer rocky islet now has two eggs; dated them.   Nest well built of sea-weed, feathers, moss and lichens.

Took two hauls of the dredge: the first in $2\frac{1}{2}$ to 3 fathoms, bottom gravel, the second in 4 to 5 fathoms, bottom gravel with clumps of weed.   Surface temperature 29°·1.   First dredge: limpets, same as the shore form; lamellibranchs of several species, including dead shells; two other species of gasteropods, the first of which is certainly a form we have not got before and probably the second also; three small isopods, all one species.   Second dredge: several species of small amphipods; chaetopods, two or three species; chitons; small lamellibranchs, numerous spawning limpets and two other gasteropods of one species.   Spawn attached to pebbles, probably of some mollusc, yellowish rounded faced tetrahedra with egg inside.

Trap in $4\frac{1}{2}$ fathoms contained two fish, one cushion-star and a very few amphipods.   Shifted it to 6 fathoms on a bottom of gravel with abundant weed clumps.

Dec. 4th.—Was at a big rookery at north-west end of Laurie Island beside Nigg Rock; entirely occupied by ringed penguins, some with two eggs, but the majority with one and some with none, so evidently they have only just commenced laying.   Coming back along the west side of Jessie Bay I got about two dozen Cape pigeons' eggs and 18 snowy petrels'.   Some Cape pigeons have not laid yet but all snowies seem to have done so.   Got ten of the latter's eggs in one cave, about 35 feet above sea level, in holes in the dung-covered floor.   These nests, unlike all others, were made either of pieces of dung or with feathers.   Some were right at the back of cave, which was about 40 feet long and almost dark.   Temperature in cave 35°.   Got four more in a similar but smaller cave.

All other usual birds seen about and no unusual ones.   Weddell seals observed.

Dec. 5th.—Took two dredgings in Uruguay Cove.   Temperature of surface between 29° and 30°.   First dredge—2 to 8 fathoms, bottom gravel with clumps of weed— contained small crustaceans; limpets, one lamellibranch and several other small gasteropods; a few pycnogons; several small worms, one like the common large nemertean, and one small chaetopod.   Second dredge—5 to 15 fathoms, gravel and mud, mainly the latter—contained a considerable number of pycnogons, two cushion-stars, several small isopods, several amphipods, and some limpets.

Got about 50 Cape pigeons' eggs on the east side of Uruguay Cove where that bay opens into Jessie Bay. All are single eggs. Eleven snowy petrels' eggs got also. Numerous terns nesting there but most have not laid, and only one egg was found. One gull's nest with three eggs which were well incubated.

A small petrel similar to a Wilson's petrel was caught. From a rock about 15 feet above the sea I heard a low whistling note, and proceeding to investigate I found in a crack what I took to be a pair of Wilson's petrels, and managed to catch one of them. Two hopelessly broken eggs were lying at the mouth of the crack, and one other one not so badly broken was brought away. It had been partly incubated. The bird was different from a Wilson's petrel, in having entirely black feet, being white on the under surface, and having feathers on back slightly tinged with white and a longer and more hooked upper mandible and a strongly up-turned tubi-nostril.[1]

In evening caught a real Wilson's petrel in the cliffs above the house where they were nesting at a height of 150 to 200 feet. Three nests were all found in small cracks or crevices in the rocks, and to reach the one I caught I had to dig away both rock and earth before I could get my arm in. All three nests contained broken, partly incubated old eggs, and in one a dead young bird was got of last or some previous year. It seems as if they returned to the same places to nest, and as if last (or some previous year) the birds had been caught by an early onset of snow which stopped incubation.

From 7 P.M. to 11 P.M. numerous Wilson's petrels may be seen flitting about the cliffs here and over the water, much more abundantly than during the day-time, when only a single one is occasionally seen.

Shags, skuas, nellies, paddies and three kinds of penguins seen about as usual. On The Beach black-throated penguins are very common, gentoos fairly common and ringed penguins rather uncommon, probably because their rookery is much further off.

Dec. 6th.—There was a very low tide to-day, so we went collecting in shore pools on the west side of the head of Scotia Bay (near the magnetic stick). Almost no weed in these pools, except for a few pieces of dulce ; weed begins in about one fathom below low-water mark. Notwithstanding this, a pretty good haul was made on and under the stones of the pools. Temperature of the pools varied from 30° to 32°, being rather warmer than the open water of the bay.

Our collections were as follows:—Four fish, small specimens of same species that is very common in the trap at about 10 fathoms; limpets, by far the most abundant of any species in the fauna, while small silvery white gasteropods ("Silver Willies") were about the next most plentiful, several other species of gasteropods and one or two small lamellibranchs ; two small nudibranchs of the same species as got in dredge from 10 fathoms ; crustaceans of numerous small forms—chiefly amphipods ; star-fish, small orange-red form pretty abundant and one yellow form, also common in 10 fathoms, one small species (about ⅜-in.) red-brown, centre fading to white at tips of arms ; one holothurian, a species common in 10 fathoms ; chaetopods, one very small form ; polyzoa, one orange-coloured calcareous form encrusting the stones in scalloped pieces,

[1] *Fregetta melanogaster.*

Zoological Log of Scottish National Antarctic Expedition.

[Photo by W. S. Bruce.

94. Giant Petrel (*Ossifraga gigantea*) Grey Variety, on Nest of Stones.

[Photo by D. W. Wilton.

95. Giant Petrel, White Variety, and Nest with Egg.

[Photo by W. S. Bruce.

96. Giant Petrels (*Ossifraga gigantea*) Pale Grey, Dark Grey, and
White Varieties, gorging on a blubber off Seal Skin.

[Photo by W. S. Bruce.

97. Giant Petrel rising with difficulty after gorging.

others on shells, rock and stalked coelenterates ; eight sea-anemones, all of one species, a kind of yellowish salmon colour, the same, I think, as has been dredged from 10 fathoms, and a stalked colonial hydrozoon, forming beards on the stones ; sponges, same form as got in 10 fathoms dredge ; pycnogons, three to four of the common small species.

First young adelia penguins were got to-day at the "Half-Moon" rookery. About a dozen hatched altogether. Probably some were hatched yesterday or the day before at the big rookery, as, when we were there on the 3rd, some of the eggs were chipped. Got dated gentoo eggs for embryos, 21 to 23 days old.

N.B.—Of the embryos preserved as being of same date, some are evidently not at the same stage of incubation although laid on same date. This is probably because an interval of two or three days has elapsed between the laying of the two eggs, and I suppose incubation has only thoroughly started after the second one was laid. If two embryos marked as being of same day of incubation are at different stages, the more advanced one will therefore be the more nearly correct, as these figures express correctly at least the maximum stage of development.

Other birds seen about were ringed penguins, skuas, nellies, gulls, paddies, terns, Wilson's and snowy petrels, and Cape pigeons. Numerous pieces of compound ascidians seen floating in the bay and also cast up on The Beach. Numerous Weddell seals on the shore about Point Martin.

Dec. 7th.—Birds seen : three species of penguins, gulls, nellies, skuas, paddies, terns, snowy petrels and Wilson's petrels.

Dec. 8th.—Birds observed : ringed and adelia penguins, gulls, nellies, skuas, shags, paddies, terns, Wilson's and snowy petrels, and Cape pigeons.

Dec. 9th.—Birds observed : black-throated penguins, gulls, skuas, terns and snowy petrels.

Dec. 10th.—Birds seen : three kinds of penguins, skuas, gulls, shags, nellies, terns, paddies, Cape pigeons, snowy petrels and Wilson's petrels.

Skua's nest on moraine above Point Martin—one egg (broken). Got gentoo penguins' embryos, 24 to 27 days old, from "Half-Moon" rookery. Not a great number of adelia young as yet. The adelia penguins are very much quieter to-day than I have ever observed them before. There is a large bare patch on the abdomen into which the chicks creep and are well protected from the wind and snow. No gentoo young at this rookery yet.

Weddell seals on the beach at Point Martin. Saw one young one with its first coat not yet all cast. They seem to be in pairs. Saw one adult going into the sea between two floe-pieces. The gap was very narrow between the ice tongues, and the seal had to lash out vigorously with it hind flippers before it could get through. We had observed a recent bleeding sore on its flank, and it was suggested that ice is a possible cause of the scars on seals.

Dec. 11th.—Down at the large penguin rookeries. Large number of young birds now but still a considerable quantity of unhatched eggs. Some of the

M

chicks certainly a day or two ahead of those at the "Half-Moon" rookeries. No gentoo young seen.

Got six skuas' eggs—all single, mostly on mossy rocks, one high up on the ridge between Scotia and Buchan Bays. To one of the skuas from whom we took an egg we gave a penguin egg, and about half-an-hour later found her sitting quite contentedly on it.

Got eleven paddies' eggs, two nests of three, two of two and one with one. The last we dated and left. Four of the nests were quite low down, between 10 and 20 feet above sea-level, and situated in crevices of the rock or under a boulder on the edge of the rookery—usually between it and the sea. Nests composed mainly of egg-shells and penguin bones, also penguin feathers and limpet-shells. One nest was well up on the large moraine rookery, a full arm's length in under a large boulder and right among the penguins. Two other nests with no eggs. Got one Wilson's petrel's egg in cliffs above the house in the same nest where I caught the petrel a few days ago.

Weddell seals on the west side of the bay as usual.

Dec. 12th.—At big ringed penguin rookery to N. N. W'. Most of the birds have laid now. Only saw one nest with three eggs and the third was an extremely small one. At mouth of Uruguay Cove on the east side, got six Cape pigeons' eggs, and one snowy's and six terns'. All the terns' were single eggs. A skua was hovering about there, seemingly on the look-out for petrels' eggs. One sucked Cape pigeon's egg was observed. No sign of the mate of the new petrel caught there a few days ago.

On rocky islet at head of Scotia Bay the shags settle every night, but there are no signs of their nesting there. A tern was seen pursuing fiercely the gull which is nesting there; reason unknown. A couple of paddies seem to be nest-building on the islet.

All birds of the islands, at least the twelve common species, observed. Lifted trap which had been down for about a week. Ice had carried it inshore a good bit; nothing in it. Replaced it in 6 fathoms on gravel and weed, and lowered the other one near the rocky shore in dense weed, 4 fathoms.

One Weddell seal seen in Uruguay Cove on a floe-piece.

Dec. 13th.—Birds: skuas, gulls, terns, Wilson's petrels, snowy petrels, paddies, adelia penguins, (?) silver petrel and nellies.

Several pieces of compound ascidian thrown up on The Beach; measured one piece, 20 feet long, and it may have been longer as another piece about 10 feet long lying beside it looked as if it had been broken off.

Dec. 14th.—Went to Point Davis. Expected to find young gulls and terns, but none are hatched yet. Caught a Wilson's petrel on nest (same nest as before), but no eggs yet. Found another old nest with a dead young bird in it. Other birds about: skuas, nellies, paddies, shags, adelia penguins and snowy petrels.

Dec. 15th.—Birds: all the twelve common species observed, and in addition a single silver petrel flying over the head of Scotia Bay.

Lifted trap, 4 to 6 fathoms, Scotia Bay. Only cushion-stars and other star-fish.

---

[1] The large rookeries about Route Point.

Dredge, 5 to 10 fathoms, gravel and mud.   One sea-urchin, one cushion-star, and one yellow star-fish, and a few pycnogons.   10 to 20 fathoms, mud, nil.   Trawl, nil; did not sink properly.

Dec. 16th.—Got last batch of embryos from little rookery.   Some half-dozen or so gentoo eggs hatched now.   Saw chipped eggs of 15th, 14th, and 13th November, and some of the hatched eggs were of these dates.   This gives a minimum incubation of 31 days.   The gentoos are a little more courageous now, but still some will desert a chick without showing fight, though others fought fiercely, more with flippers than with beak however; and decidedly hard smacks they can give with flippers.

Other birds: adelia and a few ringed penguins, skuas, gulls, nellies, terns, paddies, Wilson's and snowy petrels.

Dec. 17th.—All twelve common species of birds seen flying about except Cape pigeons.   During last week or so very few Cape pigeons have been seen flying near The Beach, but of course they can always be seen on their nests on the west side of Uruguay Cove.

Trap in 10 fathoms, mud, contained three fish, a few cushion-stars and many buckies.

Trap No. 2 seems to have been carried away by a piece of ice.

Dec. 18th.—Paddy's nest in which one egg was dated (11th) has now three eggs: left them there for future use.   Got one egg in one of the nests in which two were got on the 11th.   Found one other nest with two eggs, but unfortunately both got broken.

Adelia penguins: chicks growing rapidly.   Saw mother feeding youngsters.   She bends her head down till her bill is inclined at about 45°, with *upper* mandible *lowermost*.   Then the chicks suck up the semi-digested food, brought up from her stomach, out of the hollow between the rami of the upper mandible.

Gentoo penguins: dated eggs, 33, 34 and 35 days laid, are on the point of hatching.

Skua: the one which we saw sitting on the penguin's egg which we foisted (Dec. 11th) on her no longer does so.   The egg has disappeared.

Other birds about: ringed penguins, nellies, Wilson's and snowy petrels, terns, shags and gulls.   Two of the latter, mature birds, shot.

Seals: numerous Weddell seals on shore in south corner of Scotia Bay.   One Ross seal which we tried to get, but it stood up on its fore-flippers like a walrus, then backed in that position and fell down a crack between the ice-foot and a stranded floe, whence it could neither get out nor could we budge it.   Seemed to be a very old one from the worn state of the teeth.   Had 5 claws between 1½ and 2 ins. long on each fore-flipper.

Trawl.   Got trawl in good working order.   Had a long haul in water of 2 to 5 fathoms over varied bottom, mostly gravel and weed, but caught absolutely nothing.

Dredge.   In water ½ to 1½ fathoms deep (low tide), gravel, sand and mud. Contents:—numerous limpets, some buckies and chitons, lamellibranchs (all empty shells), fifteen small greyish isopods, some with eggs on under surface of thorax, and one red feathery species of holothurian which has also been got floating on the surface.

Insects: some small red insects on moss (acarinids).

Dec. 19*th.*—Birds about : three kinds of penguins, skuas, paddies, gulls, nellies, shags, Wilson's and snowy petrels, Cape pigeons and terns.

Dec. 20*th.*—Birds : skuas, gulls, terns, nellies, Wilson's petrels, adelia and ringed penguins.

Dec. 22*nd.*—Birds : adelia and ringed penguins, skuas and nellies.

Dec. 23*rd.*—Birds : adelia and ringed penguins, skuas, nellies, gulls, terns, Wilson's and snowy petrels, paddies and shags.

Neither the Cape pigeons' nor the gulls' nests near the house have young as yet. A dead Wilson's petrel was picked up on the snow near the house. Have not seen so many Wilson's petrels flying about lately, nor can they be seen in their nesting places where they were found first.

Had dredge down twice and caught one limpet.

Dec. 24*th.*—Young penguins got at small rookery. Birds under a fortnight old have already a small geological museum in their stomachs.

Three kinds of penguins, gulls, terns, skuas, shags, nellies, Wilson's and snowy petrels, and paddies. Weddell seals on west side of the bay.

Dec. 25*th.*—Weddell seals swimming out at the head of the bay. Adelia and ringed penguins always abundant on the ice-foot now. Skuas, gulls, terns, nellies, Wilson's and snowy petrels, and shags.

Dec. 26*th.*—Three species of penguins, gulls, skuas, nellies, terns, paddies, shags, Wilson's and snowy petrels. Weddell seals on the ice at Point Davis. Got one young gull and one young tern at Point Davis. Saw other hatched eggs but chicks were not to be seen and had probably hidden themselves, as the two we got were trying to do, especially the gull. The gull, which is about a week old, I should think, was observed to bring up a large ball of feathers; I am trying to keep it alive. It eats pieces of penguin meat from one's hand most voraciously. Cry of both young birds like that of their parents.

Trawl in 8 to 14 fathoms contained a few pycnogons.

Dredge in 14 fathoms : one limpet, one cushion-star and one spiny ascidian; but these were not bottled till 27th, when the cushion-star had "bottled" the limpet.

Dec. 27*th.*—Three species of penguins, gulls, skuas and nellies. Young gull seems to be thriving. He will not eat when shut up in his box but on the table eats penguin, bully-beef, bread, limpets, etc., greedily, and then likes some snow to slake his thirst.

Shot a young male *Lobodon* on The Beach. His coat was dark grey, almost black dorsally, but with a little mottling of lighter colour. Underneath, the colour was silvery grey with a yellowish tint and much mottling, especially near the junction with the darker dorsal strip. The mottling was not indistinct but in very definite spots, mostly small, *i.e.* 1 in. or less; flippers dark grey like back with considerable mottling; stomach and intestine empty.

Dec. 28*th.*—Paddies : got two eggs and the bird on its nest where three eggs had already been lifted. One egg in another nest where three had previously been got.

Zoological Log of Scottish National Antarctic Expedition.

[Photo by W. S. Bruce.

98. Giant Petrels, Nellies, or Stinkers (*Ossifraga gigantea*) Nesting at Cape Geddes, South Orkneys.

[Photo by W. S. Bruce.

99. Sheath Bills or Paddies (*Chionis alba*), at Ferguslie Peninsula, Macdougall Bay.

Skuas : four nests with two eggs and one with one egg on mossy rock. Left all these eggs.

Gulls : one egg—I think the second laid one—in a nest on the rocky islet (Shag Rocks), commencing to hatch (seen June 7th). This gives an incubation period of 27 days. Cape pigeons' eggs not yet hatched.

Wilson's petrels : caught one, a female, in same nest where a bird and egg have already been got. Three species of penguins, nellies, snowies and shags about.

Seals : 98 Weddell seals lying on the beach at Point Martin. About 50 more in the neighbourhood of the large rookery and several on the North Beach. No other seals seen.

Got a holothurian and a new species of crustacean floating entangled in weed on the surface.

Dec. 29th.—Three species of penguins, skuas, gulls, nellies, terns and snowy petrels. In a pool of melted snow on the North Beach several tape-worms were found. If they have not come from the dog Russ, it seems most probable that they are from the skuas, as they bathe very frequently in that pool.

Dec. 30th.—Got three young gulls at Point Davis, two of which were killed and one was picked up dead. The one we kept alive is well and lively, and blessed with a huge ever-present, omnivorous appetite. No young terns seen ; I think they must hide themselves.

Birds : three species of penguins, paddies, skuas, gulls, nellies, Wilson's and snowy petrels, shags and one Cape pigeon.

Got a small chaetopod worm swimming near the surface of the water by the shore ; seems to have eggs attached ventrally.

Examined scrapings of rocks and mud from pools on mossy rocks for diatoms, and found insect larvae (probably collembolids) and also small thread-worms.

Dec. 31st.—Birds : three species of penguins, skuas, gulls, nellies, shags, Wilson's and snowy petrels.

Weddell seals on ice in Uruguay Cove.

Jan. 1st, 1904.—Birds : three species of penguins, shags, nellies, gulls and snowies.

Jan. 2nd.—In shore pools got small nemerteans with eggs in capsules attached to them, small flat sea-anemones attached to rocks, a new species of holothurian and some small molluscs.

Went down to small rookery and got phonograph records ; good of black-throated penguins, but poor one of gentoos as the birds would not stay on their nests ; moreover this record got cracked afterwards. All other twelve species of birds except Cape pigeons.

Numerous Weddell seals on The Beach.

Dredge. 10 to 5 fathoms between spit and cairn, gravel, weed and mud. Temperature of surface 31°·5. Contained one small fish, probably of same species as the second most common one we have got, several small isopods, a new species of heart-urchin, numerous pycnogons, some small crustaceans and molluscs.

Trap. Numerous buckies, a few star-fish, and three fish of the common species.

Jan. 3rd.—Three species of penguins, skuas, gulls, nellies (three white ones out of about ten altogether), terns, shags, Wilson's and snowy petrels.

Jan. 4th.—Birds : all twelve species except paddies. Cape pigeons have no young hatched as yet. A Wilson's petrel caught in an old nest with two eggs of previous year in it, both of which had never hatched.

Several Weddell seals on the North Beach. Killed two females, one of which had an embryo only about 1 in. long. In its stomach were remains of abundant fish, some lamellibranchs, cuttle-fish beaks,[1] and a crustacean of a new species in fairly good condition. Plenty of nematodes in the stomach and tape-worms in the intestine. A bladder worm, a stage of a tape-worm, got in areolar tissue below the blubber. Other females had embryo 4 ins. to 5 ins. long. Stomach empty save of worms.

Jan. 5th.—All twelve species of birds, except paddies. Skuas very abundant, nearly 100, I should think, at seals' crans on the North Beach. Shot a white nelly, an immature gull, a tern (of which a painting was made) and a shag in apparently mature plumage, but the colouring of the eye, the wattle and the feet not well marked for painting.

Jan. 6th.—All twelve species of birds seen about.

Jan. 7th.—Whales reported blowing to westward of Saddle Island. Down at big penguin rookery. Got two fairly good phonograph records of ringed penguins. Ringed penguins hatched. Young seen, about two days old at most, but the nests we visited were not at the place where the first laid eggs were found. Young are lighter coloured than the two other species at the same age. Caught a new penguin for this locality, a yellow-crested one, probably a " macaroni."[2] It was well up on the rookery amongst a crowd of adelias. Paddies' eggs chipped but not actually hatched ; incubation therefore about 28 days. Skuas not yet hatched. Gull on small rocky islet visited ; egg noted as chipped on 28th December thrown out of nest and youngster in it dead, only about half developed. Other egg addled. Other usual birds of the locality noted.

Numerous Weddell seals along west side of Scotia Bay. On the North Beach got two sea-leopards, both females. (1.) 11 ft. 6 ins. long. Uterus empty. Stomach contained much sand, many penguin feathers and a few nematodes. (2.) 11 ft. 4 ins. long. Gut 92 feet long. Uterus empty. Stomach contained large quantity of shrimp-like crustaceans too far digested to recognise, and one set of penguin tail-feathers. Numerous worms in intestine. Both seals seemed to be in process of changing coats. The first had not proceeded far and was very indistinctly marked. The second had nearly changed and its coat was almost of a uniform length, with only a few patches of longer hair, mostly dorsal and about the head. The upper part was of darker steely-grey colour, almost black with light grey spots about 3 ins. in diameter.

Young captive gull is always alive and healthy, and is growing immensely ; his

[1] From the frequent occurrence of cuttle-fish beaks in the stomachs of Weddell and other seals, there was the strongest evidence for the existence of a large species of cuttle-fish. However, none were sighted until Señor Valette captured one, over six feet long, in March 1904, in Scotia Bay.

[2] *Catarrhactes chrysolophus.*

feathers are beginning to shed. He eats almost anything in the way of food, including matches, bits of tobacco, or, if he can get them, quantities of stones. His regular diet is penguin and some bread, but he seems fondest of fish and pebbles.

Skuas appear to eat both dead skuas and dead nellies; but nellies themselves eat neither.

Trap lifted; one small fish and one buckie.

Jan. 8th.—Birds about: three species of penguins, skuas, shags, nellies, gulls, terns, Wilson's and snowy petrels, and paddies. In the droves of penguins on The Beach by the house the ringed penguins are undoubtedly "bosses"; they "jockey" the black-throats and the few gentoos. Whales (finners) seen blowing close in in Jessie Bay.

Had dredge down—got nothing whatever in it.

Jan. 9th.—Got many collembolids on a penguin's carcase on The Beach. These insects are always to be found amongst the beach pebbles, where I suppose they can always get food in the form of little bits of animal matter thrown up by the sea.

Three species of penguins, skuas, nellies, gulls, terns and Wilson's petrels.

Jan. 10th.—Birds about: three species of penguins (ringed are now by far the most abundant on The Beach), skuas, nellies, gulls, shags, terns, Wilson's and snowy petrels.

Was up at Cape pigeon's nest above Uruguay Cove—no chicks yet.

Jan. 11th.—Traps lifted—one in 6 fathoms, two cushion-stars; one in 12 fathoms, two large isopods, several yellow star-fish and cushion-stars and some few amphipods.

Dredged several times, but caught nothing. The dredge will not work downhill and the wind is too strong to allow us to pull up against it.

Got a curious penguin on the South Beach, probably an albino *P. adeliae.*[1] Plumage a light mousey colour, darkest point under throat, beak same colour as adelia but rather a short one; eyes normal, tail white, with two extra tail feathers; feet pale both above and below. Numerous ringed penguins, a few gentoos, skuas, nellies, gulls, shags, terns, Wilson's and snowy petrels.

Got some tapes among penguin droppings on the ice-foot, most probably from *P. antarctica*—possibly however from *P. adeliae*—very improbably from *P. papua.*[2]

Jan. 12th.—Birds about: skuas, three species of penguins, nellies, gulls, terns, paddies, Wilson's and snowy petrels.

Jan. 13th.—Cape pigeons' eggs chipped and young alive inside. This makes incubation about 42 days. Curious birds these—they sit a month on their nests before laying, and just before laying they clear out for several days, and then take six weeks to hatch.

Wilson's petrels: found several more nests, some with old eggs and dead young birds. Got three whole eggs and three broken through stones getting into the nests. Nests difficult to get into, since some of the crevices where they are found are over three feet deep. Eggs seem quite fresh yet, not long incubated. All other species of birds observed about. Hourly temperature observations are being taken on a ringed penguin.

[1] This supposition has since been verified.

[2] It was since found that, while almost all specimens of *P. papua* and *P. antarctica* contained tape worms, *P. adeliae* was always free of them.

One Weddell seal (male) on the North Beach.

Jan. 14th.—All usual birds seen about except Cape pigeons. A female Weddell seal shot on the North Beach; uterus and stomach empty. A whale seen blowing out in Jessie Bay, plunging like a grampus. Got another Wilson's petrel's egg, a dead young bird and an old unhatched egg in same hole. Killed young gull to-day; it was dying, and had been unable to stand for nearly a week; it ate heartily up till last night.

Jan. 15th.—All usual birds seen about. At Point Davis no young terns to be seen and only one egg left, while only two young gulls visible. I think the majority were hidden. At Ailsa Craig a great number of ringed penguins, also paddies, Cape pigeons, Wilson's petrels, skuas, shags and nellies. The last three species were not found nesting there.

Whale (? grampus) seen blowing near Point Davis. Weddell seal shot on the North Beach; it contained an embryo. Great numbers of compound ascidians floating about the Bay.

Traps lifted: star-fish, cushion-stars, large nemerteans, a few amphipods, two isopods, one with a parasitic worm attached; but worm lost in bottling.

Jan. 16th.—All usual birds seen about.

Jan. 17th.—Down at large rookery. Caught two more crested penguins in exactly the same place as last one. Young adelias are beginning to lose their down. The rookeries are in a greater mess than they have ever been. The dirt and smell are disgusting. Young paddies with rather patchy dark brown down. Skuas not yet hatched.

One sea-leopard seen in the water; numerous Weddell seals on beach. On The Beach at the house got part of a compound ascidian with what are, I suppose, young attached—round spikelike balls like heads of sea-kale.

Jan. 18th.—Got young Cape pigeon for skin, five days old. Got also three more Wilson's petrels' eggs and one adult for skin. All other usual birds seen about. A female sea-leopard killed on North Beach, 14 feet 8½ inches long; uterus empty; stomach contained only fish remains and lamellibranch shells.

Jan. 19th.—Birds observed: all twelve common species except Cape pigeons and snowy petrels.

Jan. 20th.—Birds: three species of penguins, skuas, nellies, gulls, shags, Wilson's petrels and terns.

Lifted traps—nothing but star-fish. Had long dredge haul up-hill and caught nothing but one limpet.

Jan. 21st.—Three species of penguins, skuas, nellies, gulls and Wilson's petrels. Got several tape-worms from intestine of ringed penguins. They are short tape-worms with a cyst, developing in the outer layers of the gut in which the head of the tape is embedded whilst the body hangs out into the main gut, chiefly near the pylorus.

Jan. 22nd.—Birds: three species of penguins, nellies, skuas, gulls, terns and Wilson's petrels.

Jan. 23rd.—Same birds as yesterday : the penguins, however, have nearly all left The Beach and not a couple of dozen remain. Latterly Mossman has been noting a habit of theirs during the night-time. Up till 2.10 A.M. they lie sleeping peaceably ; then some of them wake, and, stretching up their necks, start a chorus which is kept up intermittently till about 4 A.M. by which time they are all more or less awake and on the move. But all do not keep awake and moving (either on land or sea) all day long. At any given time during the day some may be found asleep, usually on the snow, very rarely on the beach. Snowy petrels and shags have not been seen for some days now. Weddell seals seen in the water, and whales blowing to the north-west.

Jan. 24th.—Three species of penguins back again in considerable numbers to The Beach. Nellies, skuas, terns, Wilson's petrels and gulls. Smith reported seeing two entirely white birds about the size of gulls. Cape pigeons seen flying over Wilton Bay.

Jan. 25th.—Three species of penguins, nellies, gulls, skuas, terns, and Wilson's petrels, one shag and one snowy. Got more tape-worms out of both ringed and gentoo penguins, the larger in the gentoo, but both similar in appearance and situation, *i.e.* cysts mostly near the upper end of gut. No tape-worms in black-throated penguins killed to-day.

Jan. 26th.—Three species of penguins, nellies, gulls, skuas, terns and Wilson's petrels. Weddell seals swimming in Scotia Bay. Amongst roots of weed thrown up on shore of Uruguay Cove, got numerous "worms" of various kinds, also holothurians and ophiuroids.

Jan. 27th.—Black-throated and ringed penguins, nellies, skuas, gulls, terns, Wilson's petrels and one shag. Seals in both Scotia Bay and Jessie Bay.

Jan. 28th.—Got two young snowy petrels on east side of Jessie Bay, but the parent birds were not at home in either case. The birds emitted a harsh whistling note like the old ones and ejected red fluid from their stomachs just as the parents do ; stomachs crammed full of red crustaceans. A Wilson's petrel egg also found. About half-a-dozen young adelia penguins appeared on The Beach to-day, and some got as far across as the North Beach.

The note of the young bird is very like the "maa maa" of a very young lamb. Some had not entirely lost their down, and the white ring round the eye is in none of them showing more than a trace of white.

Others birds about : three species of penguins, gulls, skuas, nellies, terns, Wilson's petrels and snowy petrels.

Jan. 29th.—Visited the large penguin rookery : the great majority of the young adelias have not yet taken to the water since the casting of the down is not completed. This process commences on the breast and under parts of the body, neck and flippers, and then on the dorsal aspects, the last parts to cast being generally above the root of the tail and at the base of the flippers, and finally the crown of the head.

The young gentoo penguins have not yet begun to lose their down.

N

Noted numerous cases of the young chasing the parent bird about to get food, but the parents seem to be getting tired of the game and generally tried to run off and avoid it, though the maternal instinct proved rather strong and would urge them to stop and have compassion.

How the young get into the water we did not see, but, the plunge once taken, they are very soon left to shift for themselves, as the young birds we have seen on The Beach were sometimes unaccompanied by any adult adelia penguin. If they happened to be, the latter took no apparent interest in the youngsters.

Even on the rookeries young birds are to be seen congregated in parties of a dozen with no, or perhaps one, old bird near them. But this early turning adrift makes the young bird pay a heavy toll. Abundant remains of recently killed young ones are lying all over the place, while nellies, filled to repletion, are waddling all around and sleeping on the snow slopes above the moraine. Nemesis, in the person of a scientist, overtook one of these unwary sleeping murderers, but in return it was immortalized on a photographic film before being sent per express to join its ancestors in the happy hunting-ground where all is blood and blubber.

Scores of skuas and dozens of gulls flying in flocks about the nellies as jackals do about lions, assist in completing the tale of this Herodian holocaust, making up in numbers what they lack in rapacity.

Some of the skuas' eggs are just chipping but the majority are hatched, and the young birds, which are at the outside a week old, have already begun to wander out of the nest, and the little light-brown masses of down are very difficult to make out against the background of brown moss. Two were taken for specimens. One young paddy was taken, with the white feathers beginning to develop under the dark yellow-brown down; it would be about a fortnight old. Two more crested penguins were caught, one, an old bird, on the shore just below where the previous three were got—the other, at the same place as the previous ones, appears to be a this year's bird, from the size and immature appearance of the beak and crest. If this is so, do these birds breed in the South Orkneys or has this youngster made the long journey from South Georgia or the Falkland Islands to here at this early stage of its career?

A gull was shot which appears to be a this year's bird. Ringed penguins, terns, Wilson's petrels and a few shags also noted.

Numerous Weddell seals round the shore.

Traps lifted: two isopods; when they were put in a basin, a worm was observed which seemed like the one previously noted as parasitic on this animal, but I did not actually observe this one attached to the isopod. Also a few star-fish and cushion-stars, one polychaete and some amphipods.

Jan. 30th.—Three species of penguins, nellies, skuas, gulls, terns, Wilson's petrels and shags.

At the skuas' nests on the moraine, on the west side of Scotia Bay, we got one young bird. The skuas are not appreciably fiercer with young than with eggs, although if the dog was near by they pursued him more energetically, swooping over him and hitting him a good smack with their feet. They fly over people in the same way but never appear to hit anyone. If one stands at the nest, they keep flying around for a few minutes but soon come within a yard or two. A young gull, still completely downy, ran away from me and took readily to the water, swimming with ease.

Over 100 Weddell seals on the beach on the west side of Scotia Bay. In observing closely their coats one finds there is a great variation, no two being alike, and they seem to be in all stages of changing coats ; some even have a complete old coat, of which the hairs can easily be pulled out. Then again the colour varies greatly, and apart from actual variations it differs according to your point of view, *i.e.*, whether you look from for'ard with the lie of the hair, abeam, or from aft for'ard against the grain. When looking aft, and to a less extent abeam, there is a silvery sort of sheen which is quite awanting if they are viewed from aft. Some few were of an almost uniform creamy colour with a yellowish tinge, sometimes a greenish yellow, and in two cases a brownish yellow. In practically every one the dorsal aspect is darker than the ventral. Mottling is practically always visible, but where the old coat is complete it may be very indistinct. The amount and size of the mottling also varies very much and may take the form of small spots or of large patches. Generally speaking however, it comes to be light spots with a dark ground dorsally and dark spots with a light ground ventrally. The mottling is best seen ventrally and about the flippers, as these are the first places to cast the old coat; a broad dorsal ridge is the last region to change. The coloration of the new coat is on an average a dark slatey-grey in the dark parts and a yellowish white in the light, but the exact shades vary very much in their intensity.

Not many of these seals showed scars—only one bad case was seen and that was on a this year's seal, which had a large bare patch over the back of the skull (an unusual situation), extending the whole width of the skull—about 5 inches in width at its greatest—and it had one eye badly injured. A large proportion, both male and female, have sores (now mostly healed) about the genital organs.

Jan. 30th.—A male sea-leopard shot on the North Beach. Length, 8 feet 11½ inches ; stomach contained only a great quantity of small crustaceans.

Jan. 31st.—Three species of penguins ; young adelias now pretty abundant and many have not yet lost all their down. Nellies, gulls, skuas, terns and Wilson's petrels.

Numerous whales seen blowing to the north-west. Two Weddell seals on The Beach.

Feb. 1st.—Three species of penguins, skuas, gulls, nellies, terns, shags and Wilson's petrels.

Had three hauls of the dredge in the eastern part of the head of Scotia Bay.

First haul, 12 to 15 fathoms, shingle, weed and mud : star-fish, one heart-urchin, a large chaetopod and an annelid tube, some limpets, sea-spiders, and small gasteropods and amphipods.

Second haul, about 6 fathoms, sandy mud: several heart-urchins, some molluscs, (including a new species of brachiopod) and abundant worm-tubes.

Third haul, in similar conditions to second: a small fish, a heart-urchin, and some dead lamellibranch shells.

Feb. 2nd.—Birds: three species of penguins. An albino ringed penguin caught of a very fine white colour; parasitic insects found on it. Skuas, nellies, gulls, terns, shags and Wilson's petrels.

There being a low tide to-day we went shore-collecting. In Uruguay Cove in pools amongst boulders under the glacier face, we got a good many small amphipods, a few limpets, pycnogons and small orange coloured star-fish.

In rock pools on the west side of Scotia Bay we got numerous amphipods, a broken-off fixed tunicate, probably only washed up into the pool, several small disc-like coelenterates of the same species as already got (drawn and painted)—some were adherent to the stones and some swimming free in the pools—limpets, small molluscs (gasteropods chiefly), small orange-coloured star-fish and copepods.

Feb. 3rd.—Three species of penguins, skuas, Wilson's petrels and several flocks of Cape pigeons, the first occasion these latter have been seen for a long time.

Feb. 4th.—Three species of penguins, skuas, nellies, gulls, terns, Wilson's petrels, Cape pigeons and a flock of snowy petrels—the first of these seen for some time—and one shag.

Wilson's petrel: after dark, especially on still nights, they keep up an almost continuous noise all through the night. They make two sorts of noise, first a low whistle, short but repeated at intervals of a few seconds. I found it almost impossible to locate the birds from this note; one never seems to get any nearer it when trying to follow it up. Secondly, they utter a harsh screaming chuckle, practically the same as that of the snowy petrel. The nearest resemblance I know to it is the noise of the wooden twirling toy, known as the "corncrake." They do not indulge in the peculiar mixture of clucking and cooing that the Cape pigeons do while sitting on their nests.

Feb. 5th.—Three species of penguins, skuas, nellies, gulls, terns, Wilson's and snowy petrels. Was up at Cape pigeon's nest; youngster still in down and just a little bigger than the young snowy petrels got lately, from which it may be fair to conclude that the snowy petrels sit about the same length of time as the Cape pigeons.

Young Weddell seal on The Beach. Female sea-leopard killed on the North Beach: uterus empty; stomach contained penguin remains. It was in a half-completed state of moulting. Total length over all, 11 ft. 8½ ins.

Feb. 6th.—Four species of penguins, *i.e.*, the three ordinary species and a single specimen of the crested penguin, a young bird, again caught on The Beach. Skuas, gulls, nellies, terns, Wilson's and snowy petrels. Sea-leopard in Jessie Bay.

Feb. 7th.—Three species of penguins, skuas, nellies, gulls, terns, Wilson's and snowy petrels and shags. A young tern on the beach on the west side of Scotia Bay has

Zoological Log of Scottish National Antarctic Expedition.

[Photo by J. H. H. Pirie.

100. Black-throated Penguin (*Pygoscelis adeliæ*) Feeding its Young.

[Photo by W. S. Bruce.

101. Black-throated Penguin Rookery on Ferrier Peninsula, South Orkneys.

almost lost all its down : its plumage is now of a mottled light brown, much the same as that of young gulls.   Numerous Weddell seals on that beach.

Feb. 8th.—Three species of penguins, skuas, nellies, gulls, terns, Wilson's petrels and shags.

Feb. 9th.—Three species of penguins, skuas, nellies, gulls, terns and Wilson's petrels.

Shags : all shags seen lately have been solitary birds ; no flocks have been observed. During the last day or so no adult, but only young adelias, have been seen.   All are now putting on weight, and we are getting ringed and gentoo penguins up to 16 and 17 lbs. respectively.

Feb. 10th.—Three species of penguins, skuas, nellies, gulls, terns, Wilson's and snowy petrels.

Feb. 11th.—Four species of penguins, including one crested penguin at the usual place at the rookery.   Adelias : not a single adult bird seen at the rookery or in the bay, and very few young ones.   Gentoos : young birds do not seem to have taken the water yet, and they have only made a start to cast their down ; in one or two birds only is the white band over the head beginning to show, and the neck to darken in colour.   Ringed : young birds have almost made up on the gentoos, for the black ring was noted as appearing in one or two cases.   A very heavy surf in Uruguay Cove, and a ringed penguin had a bad time landing there, bleeding about the head, back and flippers.   They can go out easily enough, but landing is not quite so simple.

Paddies : young birds have lost most of their down and got white plumage ; they are not flying yet.   We brought back two alive.

Skuas : dark feathers appearing on the wings and along the sides of the breast.

Shags : a small flock out in the bay.

Nellies, terns, gulls, Wilson's and snowy petrels also seen.

Several Weddell seals on The Beach and one young *Lobodon.*   The skin of the latter is a very fine silvery white looked at generally, but several shades darker if looked at from behind forward as in the Weddell seal ; all new coat—no moulting, not spotted at all ventrally, but dorsally it is rather darker with small spots of silvery white ; no yellow or green tinge about it ; flippers a uniform dark mousey brown.   Had a bad scar obliquely across the middle of the back.

Feb. 12th.—Three species of penguins, skuas, nellies, gulls, terns, Wilson's petrels.

Feb. 13th.—Gentoo and ringed penguins, skuas, nellies, gulls, terns, Wilson's and snowy petrels.

Feb. 14th.—Gentoo and ringed penguins, skuas, nellies, gulls, terns, Wilson's petrels and Cape pigeons, the latter in Jessie Bay.   Return of the "Scotia."

Index

References are not given to bare records of the occurrence of a species.

ERRATA.

All through read " starfish," not " star-fish."

Page   2, footnote 1, *for* " *exocetus* " *read* " *exocœtus.*"

,,   3, Dec. 20th, *for* " dynomometer " *read* " dynamometer."

.,   12, March 2nd, *for* " buloides " *read* " bulloides."

,.   13, March 6th, *for* " pterpods " *read* " pteropods."

,,   16, footnote 2, *for* " *acutus* " *read* " *antarcticus.*"

,,   16, footnote 3, *delete* " and *Nymphon orcadense,*" *and for* " both "
          read " a."

,,   18, footnote 2, *for* " *acutus* " *read* " *antarcticus.*"

,,   20, April 22nd, *for* " cushion- and star-fishes " *read* " starfishes, including
          cushion stars."   Read similarly in other places.

,.   26, June 1st and 2nd ⎫

,,   29, June 26th   ⎬ *for* " sertularians " *read* " hydroids."

,,   33, July 18th   ⎪

,,   40, August 29th   ⎭

,,   42, Sept. 8th, line 7, *for* " like " *read* " as."

,,   43, line 29, *for* " cadmion " *read* " cadmium."

.,   47, Oct. 5th, *transpose and read* " two isopods, about twelve amphipods,
          and 156 cushion stars, one of which had four arms."

,,   61, line 23, *for* " bryozoa " *read* " bryozoon."

.,   66, Feb. 26th and 28th, *for* " *Doliolum* " *read* " *Salpa.*"

.,   67, Feb. 29th, *delete* " or *Doliolum.*"

,,   68, March 12th, after *" alcyonarian" insert* " (*Primnoisis ramosa,* n. sp.)."

,.   71, March 30th, *for* " *Doliolum* " *read* " *Salpa.*"

.,   76, April 23rd, after " *alcyonarians*" *insert* " (*Thouarella brucei,* n. sp..
          and *Paramuricea robusta,* n. sp.)."

,,   81, footnote, *for* " Thynus " *read* " Thynnus."

,,   83, July 1st and 3rd, *for* " *medusoids* " *read* " *medusæ.*"

,,   91, last line, *read* " Some small red acarinids on moss."

,, 102, Index, *for* " *Pagodronia* " *read* " *Pagodroma.*"

Plate xx.—Fig. 65, *for* " Dupturi " *read* " Daption."

,.   xxiv.—Fig. 73, *for* " *Thourella* " *read* " *Thouarella.*"

,,   xxvii.—Fig. 85, *for* " Jackass " *read* " Blackfooted."

,,   xxx.—Fig. 93, *for* " *Onychotenthis* " *read* " *Onychoteuthis.*"

Scotland to Coats Land

TRACK CHART OF THE "SCOTIA," 1902-1904, BY WILLIAM S. BRUCE, LL.D.

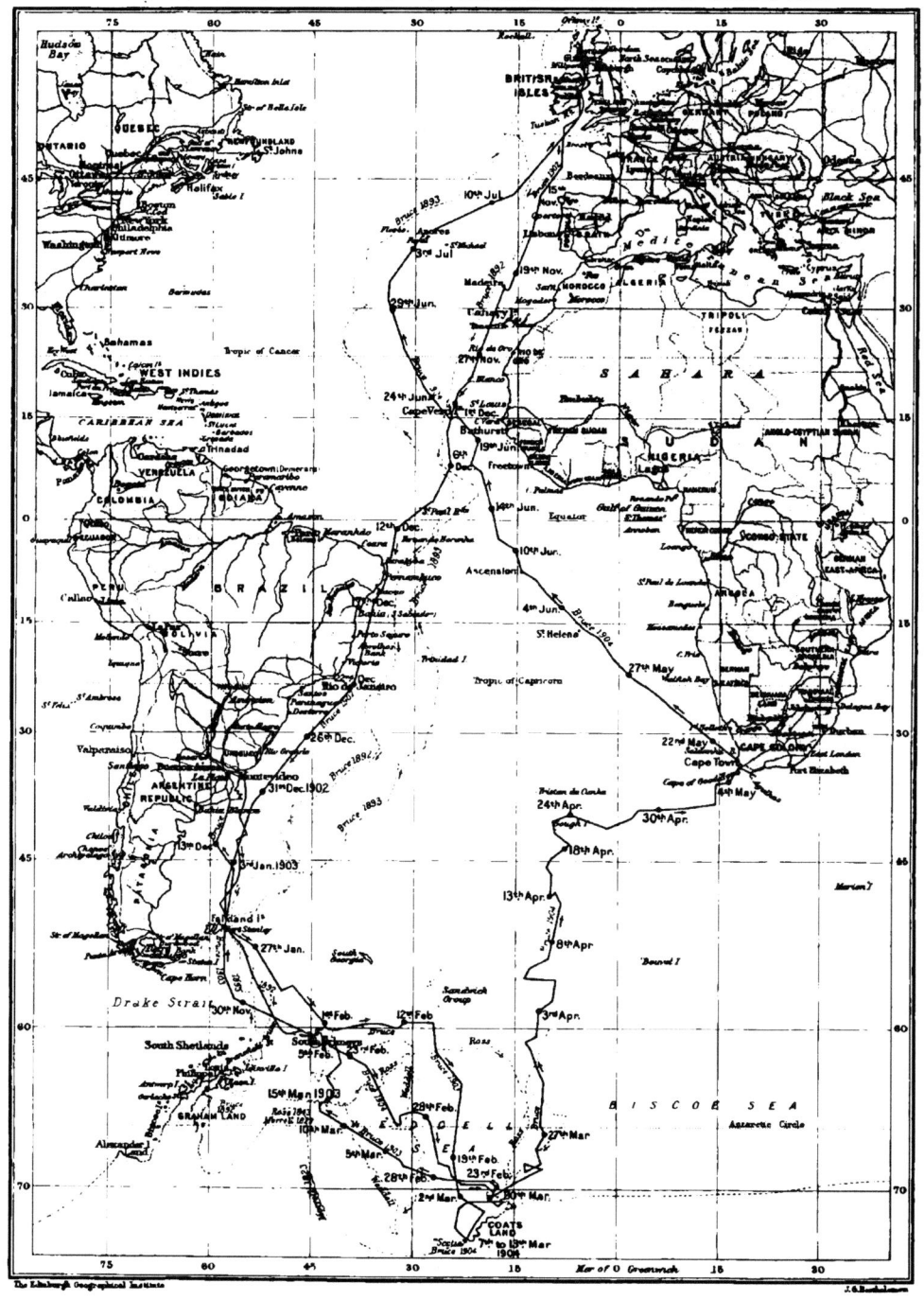

Scot. Nat. Ant. Exp. (Vol. iv., Part i.)

Zoological Log of the "Scotia."

Map II.

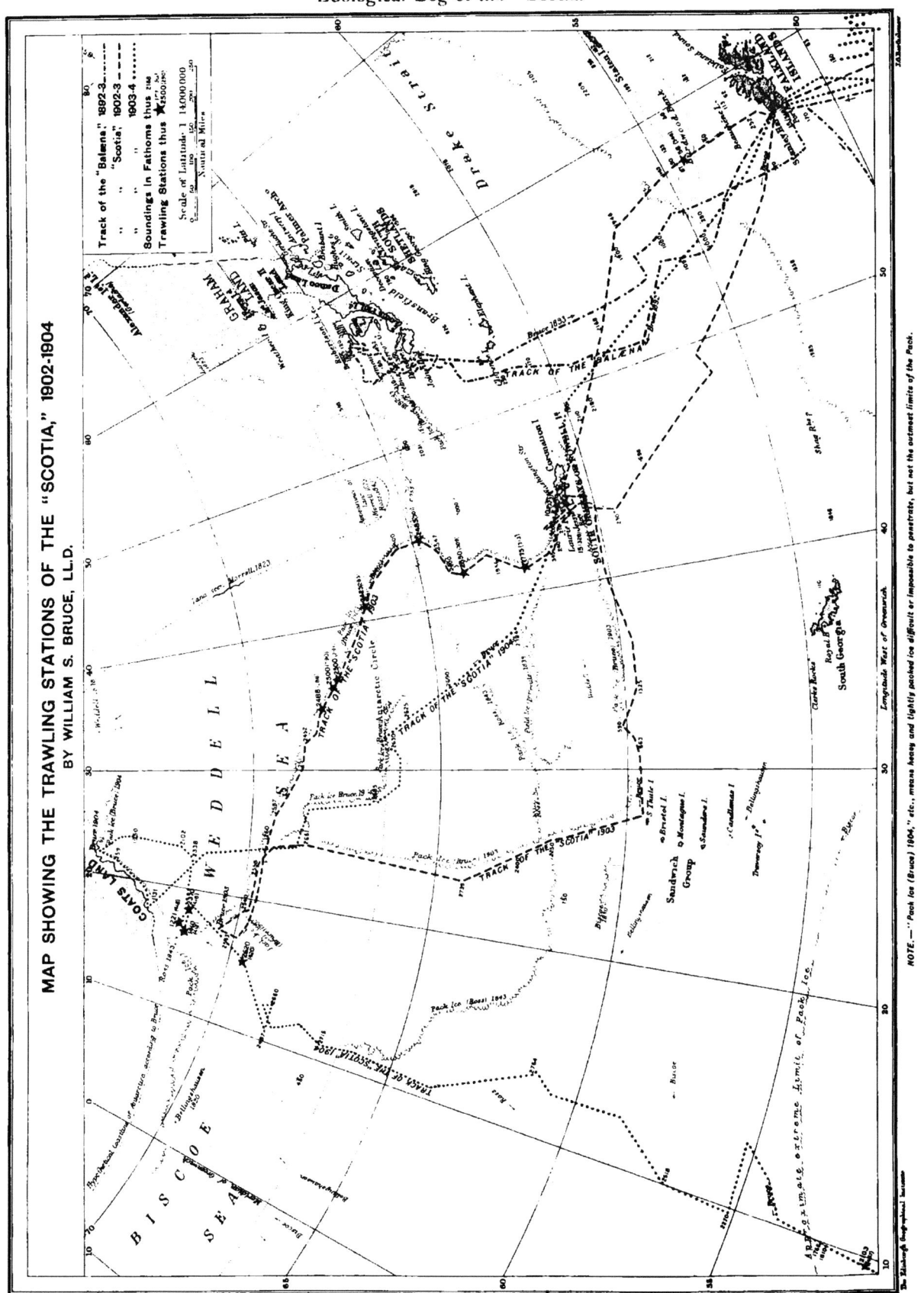

لاہور

CPSIA information can be obtained at www.ICGtesting.com
Printed in the USA
LVOW09s0028200314

378075LV00011B/569/P